The Beginner's Guide to Retirement

'You are beginning a glorious opportunity to learn, to give new things a go, be prepared to use your talents, use all of your abilities to widen your lifestyle, try everything until you are satisfied.'

Michael Longhurst

The Beginner's Guide to Retirement

Newleaf

To Paul, for the music and his unswerving adherence to what is right; and to June, who taught Mandy and I to believe in ourselves by celebrating our successes.

Published in Ireland by
Newleaf
an imprint of
Gill & Macmillan Ltd
Hume Avenue, Park West, Dublin 12
with associated companies throughout the world
www.gillmacmillan.ie

Copyright © Michael Longhurst 2000
First published in Australia in 2000 by Hodder Headline Australia Pty
Limited. This Newleaf edition is published by arrangement with Hodder
Headline Australia Pty Limited.

0 7171 3260 9

Printed by ColourBooks Ltd, Dublin

*The paper used in this book comes from the wood pulp of managed
forests. For every tree felled, at least one tree is planted, thereby
renewing natural resources.*

A CIP catalogue record for this book is available from the
British Library.

5 4 3 2

Contents

Acknowledgments

Many people gave generously of their time, assistance and encouragement during the writing of this book. In particular, I would like to give my heartfelt thanks to the following people.

Mary Drum from Hodder Headline for seeing merit in the concept and then opening the doors of Hodder to me.

Pam Brewster for providing her advice on style and layout.

Dr Prakash Nayagam of the Elm Consulting Rooms in Mornington, Victoria for his comments, additions and corrections to the chapters on diet, exercise and medical check-ups.

Julie Lane, Vesna Pavlovic and Lisa Fazio for their improvements to the chapter dealing with financial matters.

Sue Taylor for her input and suggestions.

John Murray, retired school teacher and extraordinary jazz trombonist, for his thoughts, suggestions and preparedness to provide tough criticism.

Patricia Zammit for providing her personal reactions to the book as a recently retired person.

To Ron and Fay for sharing the details of their busy schedule of activities.

Finally, I would like to thank my wife Margaret. It was her idea to incorporate additional variables into the design of the *Retire 200* research program so that this book could be written. Margaret also provided candid, no-nonsense criticism during the long writing process, and gave me the encouragement required to 'stay down the back and write' on those days when the outside world beckoned.

The reader is advised to always consult a qualified health practitioner
for psychological or health problems.

Preface

Retire 200 was an Australian research program comprising 100 men and 100 women retirees. The aim of the research was to differentiate the behaviours and activities of people who were happy with their life in retirement from those who were not. As the research progressed, it became apparent that most of the problem areas for people in retirement could be managed or removed through counselling or through the application of behavioural strategies, even where individuals had been retired for some years. This factor, combined with the encouragement of many of the participants of the *Retire 200* program, led to the writing of this book.

As each chapter of the book deals with a separate topic and is completely self-contained it is possible to go straight to the chapters that interest you most and work your way through them. The processes required to modify entrenched behaviours are clearly described so they can be applied to an individual's personal situation. Consequently, the style sometimes resembles that of a psychological text or instruction manual. As one reviewer of the book put it, 'This book needs to be read and then studied!'

The Introduction is dedicated to reporting the research findings of the *Retire 200* program. There is also a brief description of the research design process.

The remaining chapters address matters that have been found to impact on the condition of people in retirement. Each chapter examines:

◆ the retirement-related issue (for example, staying active, dealing with depression) in light of the research findings of the *Retire 200* program and of other recent social research; and

◆ practical methods for addressing the issues.

I hope you enjoy the book and find it helpful. Your observations and suggestions for improvement or addition are welcomed. I can be contacted at: PO Box 112 Mount Eliza 3930 or by e-mail at: mike_longhurst@yahoo.com

Michael Longhurst
Consulting Psychologist

Introduction

Some people thrive in retirement; each day brings new joys and new adventures to this, one of the happiest times of their lives. The responsibilities of raising families have ended, mortgages have been paid and it is *their* time to do their own thing. For others, however, retirement can be a time beset with depression, fear, anxiety and a sense of futility. It is as if all meaningful life has ended, and boredom has become entrenched.

What are the differences between these two groups of people? More importantly, what do happy people do in retirement that unhappy people do not?

The issue of retirement

There are many factors that most people can *guess* impact on satisfaction with retirement. For example, what sort of activities do people choose when they have retired? Do they sit around reading all the books they had wanted to read when they were too busy? Do they involve themselves in activities such as sport or voluntary work? Is doing all the fishing one has dreamt of doing the way to go, or is it better to lead a life with more structure and challenges?

In addition to what people *do*, it has long been thought that the circumstances surrounding *why* they retired have a significant impact on their emotional well-being. Did you retire of your own free will, or were you pushed into retirement by forces outside your control? How long does it take you to deal with the transition from full-time work?

Have you thought about how you are going to maintain your levels of fitness and mobility as you grow older? Will 'having too much time on your hands' lead to problems such as loneliness, depression or substance abuse?

Given that even modest lifestyles require income, will you have suffi-cient money to enjoy your retirement? Having to watch every cent you spend so that you have enough money for food and shelter does not seem fair when you have worked hard all your life yet, if provision is not made for retirement through superannuation or personal investments, then this penny-pinching may become a reality.

The findings of the *Retire 200* program

The objective of the *Retire 200* program was to build on earlier research from the United States and Australia to answer the above questions, and to identify the behaviours that differentiated successful retirees from their less happy peers. Having identified the behaviours of successful retirees, other retirees could then be advised to consider adapting their own behaviour to improve their satisfaction with life.

The sample of retired people studied in the research comprised 100 men and 100 women drawn from rural and urban areas of each Australian state, and from a cross-section of pre-retirement occupations. Participants in the program were volunteers recruited to the research via radio and the print media, and from notices on the bulletin boards of retirement organisations.

Designing effective social research is a complicated process. For exam-ple, if the research had comprised male retirees only, you would expect to get a one-sided view of what life in retirement is really like. As most retired couples will tell you, the roles of husband and wife often change considerably after retirement—any researcher who sought the views of just one sex would almost certainly miss the full picture. Unfortunately, much of the past research has focused on the male view of life in retire-ment and has consequently tended to present an incomplete view of retirement reality.

It is also important to ensure that the people being studied do not all come from the same geographical area, or from similar incomes or occupations. If the general public are to draw meaningful conclusions that they can apply to their own lives, it is important that those participating in the research also comprise a representative sample of society.

As mentioned earlier, the aim of the research was to differentiate the behaviours of those participants on the program who had adjusted well to retirement from those for whom retirement was a less happy experience. The degree to which a participant was regarded as 'well adjusted' to retirement was based on a combination of:

◆ their levels of retirement-related anxiety

◆ their levels of retirement-related depression

◆ their levels of retirement-related stress, and

◆ their levels of 'comparative global satisfaction'—that is, their satisfaction with life in retirement when compared with life before retirement.

Eight areas were found to impact significantly on the degree to which participants adjusted satisfactorily to retirement:

1. Being able to retire of your own free will.

2. Being able to retire at age 55 or younger.

3. Being financially independent.

4. Engaging in 'purposeful activities' for more than five hours per week.

5. Having someone on whom you could rely for emotional support.

6. Pro-actively maintaining health through exercise, diet and regular medical check-ups.

7. Planning for retirement—both financially and for an active lifestyle.

8. Receiving pre-retirement advice or education.

The following information provides a more detailed description of what each of these findings mean for those who have retired or who are about to retire.

Research Finding One:
Being able to retire of your own free will.
'Jumping versus being pushed'

The attitude you have when approaching retirement usually relates to the degree to which you can control how and when you retire. Even where everything goes the way you plan it, the decision-making period is usually a stressful and emotional time. It can also be a frightening time for those close to the retired person who may worry about how the changed circumstances will affect all concerned.

Most stories in the media about the effects of organisational mergers and downsizing focus on the immediate financial hardships experienced by those who have been retrenched, and on their efforts to regain employment. However, for many older people retrenchment also means involuntary retirement, and there is little doubt that many of those whose life plans are interrupted by forced retirement carry the effects of their pain well into retirement.

> *'I was speaking with a man who had been retrenched from his job at the age of 61 due to the downsizing of the organisation he worked for. It was now three years on and he had long since ceased looking for another job. His investments were such that he really had no need to work for an income and now regarded himself as retired from the workplace. During his lifetime he had seen the horrors of war, had run a business during tough economic times, and was a diligent and intelligent administrator for the firm that eventually retrenched him. Yet, despite having survived so many personal challenges, he was cut to the quick by the circumstances of his forced retirement. Frequently during conversations he would refer to his retrenchment as the time "they gave me the chop" and many of those around him suspected that he never really managed to get this hurt out of his system.'*

The hurt experienced after forced retirement is very common. Although there may be many reasons that drive organisations to downsize, those on the receiving end often feel that their own personal make-up or work performance caused them to be singled out. These feelings can be exacerbated when the retrenched person later sees colleagues who they regarded as less talented or less dedicated stay on with the organisation and appear to prosper.

At a psychological level, involuntary severance from one's livelihood can result in a sense of loss and a need to grieve in much the same way we do following the loss of a friend or relative. If the retrenched person closely identified with their job, they may find themselves suffering more than those for whom work was just a means to an end. If untreated, the negative impacts of this stress on their emotional well-being may persist for many years.

Consequently those people who retire voluntarily are more likely to be better adjusted to retirement and less prone to psychological stress than those forced to retire due to personal illness, the illness of a family member, retrenchment or business closure.

These findings were supported by an earlier piece of Australian research in which voluntary retirees experienced significantly lower levels of stress, anxiety, depression and bad health than those who were forced to retire. Other studies in the United States also found that retiring according to one's plans increased the likelihood of satisfaction with the experience of retirement.

The findings are disturbing given the present trends of restructuring and merging. The increasing moves to flatten organisational structures, lower staff numbers due to technology and outsource business services are resulting in increasing numbers of people being forced to retire against their will. Consequently, forced retirees need to be aware that they may be at risk from emotional health problems and should seek counselling where necessary.

Interestingly, research into organisational stress indicates that those senior managers who make the decisions regarding which people are to be retrenched themselves experience anxiety that may continue for many years. Part of their stress is attributed to their inability to explain to those who were retrenched that the 'hit lists' often had nothing to do with the individual performance of the employee. One former manager in the

Retire 200 research stated, 'I sometimes wished that I could show some of my retrenched colleagues how much thought and agonising took place before we arrived at our decisions. I am sure it would have helped soften the blow for many of them!'

Research Finding Two:
Being able to retire at age 55 or younger.
The impact of our age at retirement

Anecdotal evidence has long suggested that most people hold strong views concerning their preferred age of retirement. An informal survey conducted just before the *Retire 200* research commenced indicated that most people presently regarded as 'pre-retirees' (that is, aged 45–55) wished to retire as close to age 55 as was financially possible. Only a few on the survey indicated that they wanted to work until the traditional retirement age of 65, with most people stating that only dire financial necessity would drive them to work past the age of 65.

Interestingly, many of those 'preferring to retire at age 55' modified their definition of retiring to mean 'retiring from their present job or employer', indicating that retirement would just signify a change of occupation. They could then embark on activities of their own choice such as voluntary work, part-time work in a low stress environment, or starting their own small business.

Following the results of the preliminary informal survey, it came as no surprise that those people who were able to retire at age 55 or earlier had lower levels of anxiety than those retiring later. These findings suggest that those people who can retire at age 55 should at least consider this option, providing of course that other aspects of their lives such as financial preparedness make this a viable option.

Many people told stories of their father's generation of retired men who had worked to the age of 65 only to die a short time later. These people described themselves as haunted by the memories of hard-working relatives who had passed away just as it was time for them to relax and to do what they liked.

Others told stories of fathers so firmly committed to the work ethic and to their need to perform the role of provider that when it came time to retire, they simply could not relax. It was impossible for them to accept that it was now okay to do what they liked with their day. It was actually more stressful to 'relax' than it had been to work hard, even where their previous occupation had been intrinsically unsatisfying.

Many people found retiring at age 55 appealing because it allowed them to embark on chosen activities and personal challenges while they were still relatively young and healthy enough to do so. Many of these people told stories of parents or relatives who had planned extensive trips at age 65 only to have to cancel their plans because of the unexpected ill-health or death of one partner.

At a social level, the impact of early retirement is a double-edged sword. On one side, those retiring early from full-time work free up jobs and promotions for younger people still in the throes of raising families and paying off mortgages. Moreover, early retirees also have significant contributions to make to society in the form of voluntary work.

On the down side, it is likely that growing trends away from lifelong employment will result in people being employed in a variety of short-term contracts and consultancies. If this trend continues, only those who are well organised will commence and maintain the forced savings programs such as superannuation and personal investments which are required to fund a comfortable retirement. Furthermore, it is becoming increasingly unlikely that the present age pension can continue to be taken for granted by the growing pool of baby-boomers, funded as it will be by shrinking numbers of full-time employees.

Research Finding Three:
Being financially independent.
Comfort versus subsistence

At an intuitive level, most people would realise that those who can live from their own investments or superannuation are probably going to be more satisfied with life in retirement than those who have to rely on a government pension.

The research findings indicated that people who were dependent on government pensions for their income experienced significantly higher levels of depression, anxiety and stress and lower levels of satisfaction with life in retirement than those who were financially independent. Earlier studies also found poor financial status to be a predictor of stress and anxiety in retirement.

The age pension was regarded by most as being barely adequate to provide the basics of life. Only those who were completely debt free and prepared to live extremely simple lifestyles were able to live on the pension with any success.

Living on the age pension forced people to become very creative when it came to reducing their living costs. Some people had almost turned the process into an art form and had developed a number of strategies for getting by; for example, one woman and her husband collected discarded supermarket receipts that had special offers on the back such as 'two meals for the price of one' at the local hotel. Having had their two-for-one dinner in the main lounge they would go to the gaming section, not to gamble, but to finish their meal with the free coffees and after-dinner mints provided for the gambling patrons.

Those who found themselves on the pension while still paying off home mortgages were usually in a precarious financial position. Carrying debt into retirement occurred for a number of reasons, including:

◆ A disastrous second marriage entered into while on the rebound from the death of a lifelong partner. The resulting divorce required them to refinance their home late in life to buy out their estranged partner's interest in the house.

◆ Borrowing against the security of homes to help adult children in trouble with drugs or personal debts, or who were trying to escape abusive relationships.

◆ Falling into debt due to failed businesses where the family home had comprised the lender's security.

Simple decisions about whether or not to participate in social events were complicated by a lack of money. In a number of cases, men complained that staying back 'for a couple of beers' after bowls or golf was out of the question — they simply could not afford it. One man described himself as feeling like a child again having to ask his partner's permission to spend a few dollars. Others found it embarrassing to have to give excuses for not attending social events because of their lack of income.

For those who became ill or infirm, financial dependency left them feeling frightened and vulnerable to what they felt were the whims of an uncaring health system. Relying on the public health system may not be an issue when we are young, however, as we become older we may find ourselves suffering from a range of potentially life-threatening complaints such as hypertension, diabetes or heart disease. It is understandable to feel threatened by the inability to nominate where, when and with whom required medical procedures or advice are sought.

A number of people described the fortnightly indignity of running out of money one or two days before pension day and being forced to subsist on rice or potatoes until the next pension payment was received. This situation was by no means rare and it is a sobering experience to listen to someone describe how demoralised they feel each time the money runs out. The situation can be compounded when adult children who could and would provide assistance are blissfully unaware that their proud parent is suffering in silence.

The ability to contribute to society and mix with others through voluntary work was also denied to many people who were struggling to make ends meet on the pension. Voluntary work usually ends up costing the volunteer money in the form of petrol or fares and many could not afford these extra costs.

Research Finding Four:
Engaging in 'purposeful activities' for more than five hours per week.
'The spice of life'

It makes sense that those who keep themselves busy will fare better emotionally than those who lie around doing nothing. Further to this, if activity has a purpose it is more rewarding than activity for the sake of 'something to do'.

'Purposeful activity' was the term used in the *Retire 200* study to describe an activity that had a goal or purpose. For example, playing golf was not regarded as a purposeful activity regardless of what most golfers would argue! However, voluntary work in an opportunity shop to raise money for the Brotherhood of Saint Laurence or working in a paid capacity to supplement retirement income were examples of purposeful activities.

Involvement of over five hours per week in a purposeful activity, or a range of these activities provided significantly higher levels of satisfaction with life and lower levels of depression and stress. Participating in activities was a behaviour that retirees either planned for before retirement or sought after retirement due to boredom. Therefore, those retirees who found their lives lacking variety or purpose could embark on purposeful activities virtually any time during their retirement years.

Eighty-six per cent of those in the program regarded involvement in a purposeful activity as being very important to their satisfaction, the beneficial effects showing a positive trend even where participation exceeded 30 hours per week. These findings imply that many of the social and emotional rewards previously provided by the workplace can also come from purposeful activities in retirement, a notion supported by the fact that income was cited as the sole motivation for their involvement in an activity by only 2 per cent of participants.

Research Finding Five:
Having someone on whom you could rely for emotional support.
Availability of 'a shoulder to cry on'

> *'Keep emotionally close to your family—some people forget their family while they are traipsing around the country.'*

The level of emotional support accessible to *people who required it* was investigated for two reasons:

◆ For many people, the workplace provides a source of informal counselling where workmates discuss events going on in their lives and provide each other with emotional support during times of crisis. On retirement, these social networks disappear virtually overnight.

◆ As we get older the statistical probability that we will suffer from ill health or that our partner or a friend will become ill or pass away increases. When any of these events occurs it is important to have a shoulder to cry on, and to have people to turn to for extended emotional support.

Those with access to emotional support reported significantly lower levels of stress and higher levels of satisfaction with life in retirement, a finding that supports earlier research where availability of emotional support from family or others was associated with lower levels of anxiety and depression. Retirees should maintain their relationships with family and friends wherever possible. Those without access to such emotional support are advised to compile a list of alternative resources such as religious institutions, municipal counselling services or telephone-based crisis-referral organisations such as Lifeline.

Research Finding Six:
Proactively maintaining health.
Self-promoted health activities

While earlier research indicated that poor health is an important factor influencing satisfaction in retirement, there has been very little research on the effects of pro-actively contributing to one's good health. Consequently, *self-promoted* health activities were examined for their effect on satisfaction with retirement. Health activities were segmented into three 'sub-sets', namely exercise, diet and annual check-ups.

Those who exercised daily had significantly lower levels of stress than those not exercising or exercising less frequently. There are well-established links between high levels of emotional stress and heart attack and stroke. This is important information as many participants reported that their greatest health-related fears were heart attack, stroke and the onset of Alzheimer's disease.

Those who moderated their diet by the amount or type of food consumed were found to experience significantly lower levels of depression than those who did not attend to dietary matters. This finding is consistent with research into depressive illnesses which has found that those who attempt to take even very small steps to control their situation improve faster than those who just passively rely on others.

Those who regularly attended to all three of the sub-sets of health maintenance (exercise, diet and annual check-ups), had significantly lower levels of depression than those who attended to only one or two sub-sets.

Research Finding Seven:
Planning for retirement.
Finances and lifestyle

When it comes to planning behaviour, it seems that we generally fall into one of two categories:

◆ those who are naturally goal- and strategy-oriented and who are therefore more likely to have action plans in place to meet their goals; and

◆ those who are naturally unplanned and who prefer to live life as it comes.

Those who have not planned for their retirement are less likely to be financially prepared than those who have. However, what was not known before the research was whether planning for retirement lifestyle and activity would also result in a more satisfying life emotionally.

Those who planned for their retirement had significantly lower levels of self-reported stress, anxiety, and depression and higher levels of satisfaction with life in retirement than those who did not. These findings confirmed earlier studies that indicated significant associations between pre-retirement planning and retirement satisfaction and between insufficient pre-retirement planning and increased pre-retirement anxiety.

Interestingly, the research findings demonstrated that it was not just *financial* planning that is relevant; it is just as important to make plans for the type of lifestyle you wish to have. For example, many of those on the *Retire 200* program observed that planning for activities well before retirement had made the transition much less of a jolt. Their rationale was that if you became involved in a number of activities before you retired, then there were more common factors linking your 'pre-retirement life' to your life in retirement.

Research Finding Eight:
Receiving pre-retirement advice or education.
The benefits of a 'sneak preview'

People commencing retirement usually do so with little objective knowledge of what that lifestyle will entail, partly because there has been very little accurate information on the effects of retirement lifestyles readily available to the public. Consequently, when people commence retirement they often do so with the expectation of a lifestyle that may have very little to do with reality.

Given the lack of readily available information, people approaching retirement have little choice but to turn to friends and relatives who have already retired to try to get a snapshot of how their lives may change. The problem with this is that people's values and expectations vary widely—what may be a satisfying retirement lifestyle for one person may turn out to be unsatisfactory for another.

The perception of life in retirement may be based on a rosy existence that is predicated more on escaping from a dreary occupation than it is on looking forward to an exciting new phase in life. It was therefore decided to examine what effect receiving formal pre-retirement advice or training would have on perceptions and on subsequent emotional well-being.

The research findings indicated that those who sought pre-retirement advice or who attended pre-retirement training programs had significantly lower levels of depression than those who hadn't received this preparation. These findings supported earlier research that found that pre-retirement education provided greater retirement satisfaction and well-being and significant positive attitudes to life.

SECTION I:

Personal fulfilment and growth in retirement

'The minute you stop moving forwards you start going backwards.'

The need for continual growth and improvement is well established in business, in scientific research and in sporting circles, just to mention a few. There is no doubt that the same rule applies to our need for personal growth through having a challenging lifestyle when we retire.

Before each participant of *Retire 200* was accepted into the program it was necessary to explain to them how the research would work, what their involvement would be, and to answer any questions they had about the process. During these preliminary conversations with each participant it became apparent that the people with the most positive attitudes to life seemed to be those who were most heavily involved in an active retirement. This perception was later confirmed during the psychological assessment of each research participant.

At the top end of the scale of retirement satisfaction were those people who regarded retirement as an adventure, and who were involved in regular activities that were either creative or which involved the production of goods or services. Conversely, participants who were depressed or anxious tended to be those for whom retirement was an inactive experience, with few or no interests or hobbies beyond the daily routine of home maintenance.

The need for what is called a 'purposeful activity' was one of the central findings of the study when it came to predicting satisfaction with life in retirement. Chapter 1 focuses on this important topic.

Chapter 1

Remaining challenged and involved

The aims of this chapter are to:

◆ understand the relevance of purposeful activities to satisfaction in retirement;

◆ consider your own situation and to determine whether you could benefit from pursuing purposeful activities;

◆ provide a resource list of potential activities and contacts to pursue.

The topic of staying active was of great interest to most of the participants in the *Retire 200* program and many had strong opinions they were keen to see reported. Consequently, in this chapter there will be numerous quotations from research participants concerning their personal motivation for staying active.

The 'honeymoon' period

'Think carefully about the timing of your retirement—you feel euphoric at first but you need to have something to do.'

Anyone who has retired comparatively recently may be saying, 'But I've been retired for three months now—playing golf or fishing four times a week is all I'll ever need to do to keep *me* happy!' However, while this may seem true during the early stages of retirement, it is now well established that people typically commence a 'honeymoon' phase immediately after retiring during which time the euphoria results in retirees feeling as if they have just commenced a long holiday.

Sociologist R.C. Atchley first investigated the retirement honeymoon phase in the 1960s. He found that the honeymoon phase typically lasted anywhere from a couple of months to one year from the start of retirement. Closely linked to the honeymoon phase is the common tendency of people to find that their attitudes to life fluctuate from positive to negative for up to five years after commencing retirement.

During the honeymoon period leisure activities may well be all that you require to remain satisfied, probably because it takes most people about twelve months to work through the range of activities they were looking forward to doing when they retired. Consequently, people who have loved golf all their lives may find that eighteen holes of golf five days a week is fine for a year or so but that, eventually, the unfettered access to their sport becomes less satisfactory.

Some other retirement 'honeymoon' behaviours that were identified during the research program included:

- deciding to do little but read all the books you have always wanted to read;
- looking for a new house;
- moving to a new state;
- going on a planned trip overseas or around Australia;
- buying a new car;
- renovating or painting the house; and
- setting up a hobby room or workshop.

Of course, many of these activities really do need to be completed. Many people choose to renovate their home soon after retiring and such activities can be both practical and realistic. However, the fact remains that where such projects are commenced immediately after full-time work has ceased, the realities of life are in a sense 'put on hold'. Newly retired people find themselves pleasantly distracted and kept occupied as they plan for and complete their project. It may not be until after these projects are completed that it dawns on them that their retirement years have now started! This realisation signals the end of the honeymoon period and it is then quite common for people to enter periods of depression, anxiety or stress. This can be a puzzling and frightening experience for those who were anticipating a carefree existence.

'If you have been dedicated to your work you will flounder for the first year.'

There is considerable evidence to suggest that the intensity and duration of the honeymoon phase is linked to the level of satisfaction experienced in pre-retirement work life. If you found your work boring or were unhappy in your occupation, then retirement is more likely to be based on the need to 'escape' from work rather than on the transition to life in retirement. This can make the onset of emotional problems such as depression doubly perplexing for those who had looked forward to life in retirement for many years.

What are purposeful activities?

It became clear from *Retire 200* that there were three levels of activity undertaken.

◆ No activities: apart from the daily routine of eating, sleeping, shopping, watching TV, reading etc.

◆ Leisure activities: such as gardening, fishing, golf etc.

◆ Purposeful activities: where something is produced, achieved, or where a service is provided.

As an example of a purposeful activity many people cited gardening. For some, the principal motivation for gardening activities was not just related to essential maintenance but also to reduce grocery costs through growing their own produce. Some regarded gardening as a highly pleasurable pastime that provided the same type of release from stress found in meditation and other hobbies. Others were motivated by the prospect of entering gardening competitions such as developing new strains of roses or growing the largest pumpkin. One woman established a very large garden that she dedicated to the memory of her husband and which was open to the public. In each of these cases, gardening was regarded as a purposeful activity because it was clearly linked to a secondary goal. However, just mowing the lawn or weeding the garden to stop it taking over the house was not regarded as a purposeful activity but rather as a maintenance exercise such as cleaning or painting.

Other examples of purposeful activities are paid or voluntary work, craft or artistic hobbies, renovating a house, undertaking study or short courses, active membership of service organisations or clubs such as PROBUS.

The impact of purposeful activities

The links between low levels of depression in people who are purposefully active are supported by existing psychological research into clinical depression. It is well established that even where people have serious levels of depression, making the decision to be active usually results in some improvement in emotional well-being. It is therefore not surprising that people sometimes describe how they were depressed while inactive during their early retirement phase, but that this depression lifted once they commenced purposeful activities. Similarly, others found that they became depressed after a club or organisation that had been their focus closed for some reason. When they resumed their activities through another source, the depression lifted.

As a group, those people who spent five hours or more per week involved in purposeful activities were less depressed, less anxious, less stressed and more satisfied with their general experience of life in retirement.

As the *Retire 200* study progressed, a wide pattern of time spent in activities emerged. Some people had no structured activity to occupy their time and tended just to potter around. Others were active for many hours per week—in one case, a Tasmanian retiree was involved in activities that totalled a staggering 80 hours per week! The average number of hours per week was 23 hours for males and 17.3 hours for females. Interestingly, the closer the hours per week approached those previously spent at work, so did the trend move towards lower stress, lower anxiety, lower depression and higher satisfaction with life in retirement.

The research results indicate that having a purposeful activity in retirement is not just some form of minor distraction—it is a significant component of a well-balanced, happy retirement!

Motivation for involvement in purposeful activities?

When the information supplied by the research was examined it became clear that there were fifteen distinct reasons that motivated people to become active in retirement:

1. The desire for status.
2. The desire for creativity and production.
3. The desire for an interest.
4. The desire for having goals.
5. The desire to plan.
6. The desire to 'run the business I've always wanted'.
7. The desire to replace work.
8. The desire for balance.
9. The desire for structure.
10. The desire to be busy.
11. The desire for fun.
12. The desire for mental and physical stimulation.
13. The desire to mix with people and create social networks.
14. The desire for adventure.
15. The desire to produce income.

Not surprisingly most of these motivators, which are examined in more detail below, have also been found to impact positively on job satisfaction in the workplace. In other words, having purposeful activities in retirement can provide many of the same rewards that involvement in a satisfying work environment provided when you were engaged in the full-time workforce.

The desire for status

Status is often found near the top of the list of motivators of job satisfaction. Consequently, organisations around the world endeavour to create status symbols that will help them produce the best work environment for retaining and motivating their employees.

The desire for status can be very high for some individuals. For those who have retired, the loss of their previous occupation may also mean the loss of status. In some cases, this may not be a company-provided car or a notebook computer, but rather the status of full-time employment and all it represents in society.

'If you have been in a profession you have status—when you retire you need to hang on to being a person "of value".'

This comment came from a retired doctor who had built up a substantial practice while also holding the position of Chairman of the Board of a large private hospital. Soon after he retired, he and his wife sold their inner city home and moved to a property in the country. Their income from investments was substantial and their health was excellent but they were now both 'unknown' in their new town. The former greetings and constant recognition in the street that had once bordered on the intrusive were now missed and the doctor soon found that he was experiencing moderate depression.

Some months after the research program concluded, the doctor rang to say that he had commenced working as a locum for a couple of days a week and that his wife was now involved in charity work. Community involvement and its attending status had returned to their lives and they were happy again.

Similarly, people involved in purposeful activities can find that important and visible roles such as being the club treasurer or arranging scheduling for the delivery of meals-on-wheels can provide the status formerly provided by their full-time occupation.

The desire for creativity and production

'Have a hobby where you actually produce something—not just golf. I have seen friends retire without an activity and they die!'

'Get a hobby—preferably a creative one, not just knocking a golf ball around. You need to see something for your work.'

As indicated already, the dream of some people to spend their retirement playing golf or going fishing often fades once the novelty wears off. It is clear that having a purposeful activity with a creative component is very important to some people. The sense of achievement gained from doing something creative can represent the driving force behind a person's commitment to activities, and the choice is limitless. Some participants in the research who had an interest in woodwork or metalwork built furniture and other items that they either used themselves or gave to family and friends. Others donated their products to charities, or sold them at markets or to specialist retailers. One man with an engineering background and a large workshop produced a flywheel for use in a community project to restore an old steam engine.

The desire for an interest

'You need to seek out an interest or activity, for example, investing on the stock exchange.'

'Retirement gives the freedom to choose activities but you need to have a notion of how you are going to spend your time—what activities you will choose.'

The two quotations above highlight an interesting difference in the way people viewed their newfound freedom from full-time employment: some regarded free time as something that they desperately needed to fill with activity and were concerned that they might have difficulty finding enough to do, while others approached retirement with the view that there were many options—you simply needed to select the best from the range available. Such people would express their exasperation at some of their peers who complained that they were bored, noting that in their own case they had trouble finding enough time to do all the things they wanted to during the week!

The desire for having goals

'The flexibility of retirement can bring on a mañana mindset—you still need to plan, that is, to have goals to achieve.'

'You have got to have a definite idea of how you will spend your time when you retire—you need to have a goal to achieve.'

'Have a reason to get up each morning—have a goal for that day, especially one involving social contact.'

'Have more goals in retirement than when you were at work—join local groups.'

'Project your activities and plans well into the future—have a goal or an outing to look forward to.'

'Have plans, goals.'

Later in the book the impact of your personality and those of others on your life in retirement will be examined. However, for the time being it may be helpful to understand that about half the population is naturally inclined to set goals, while the other half prefers to be spontaneous and take life as it comes. Regardless of your personality most people enjoy having an activity to look forward to, and it was this aspect of planning that many people felt was critical to their enjoyment of life. Consequently, a number of people used a wall calendar in a prominent place in the kitchen on which they recorded future events such as club meetings, lunch with a friend, visiting the grandchildren or a trip inter-state. Being able to see a range of activities and interests stretching out into the future was their psychological buffer against any feelings of aim-lessness.

The desire to plan

'Plan well in advance what you are going to do—think about what interests you want to continue or develop.'

'Plan—think about what you are going to do.'

'Prepare for retirement—make sure you have a lot of interests. Don't put your feet up—don't move into idleness. Make sure that you have enough money to support your interests.'

'Plan things—travel.'

Closely linked to the need to have goals is the need to plan. Essentially, the difference between the two is that having a goal represents the 'destination', while planning involves designing the logistics of 'how you are going to get there'.

Planning, which continues to be important throughout retirement, includes planning finances so that there is money available for a holiday, planning where you will go on your holiday, and planning what you will do while you are away.

Planning also removes the great fear of many that inertia will overtake them. By having clearly stated goals, they felt they were less likely to fritter away their time in idleness.

The desire to 'run the business I've always wanted'

Several people, particularly those who had spent a lifetime employed by someone else, were keen to try running a small business. While the desire to bring in additional retirement income was a significant motivator in some of these cases, there were also other reasons that were just as important:

◆ There was the desire of some people to prove to themselves that they had 'what it took' to build a small business into a successful profit-making venture. In many cases, the pleasure gained from achieving even small successes far outweighed the benefits gained from the income itself.

◆ There was the keen sense of involvement gained from planning, and then executing the plan, as they ran their new business.

◆ There was the social contact that was intrinsic to the running of many businesses as the business owners interacted with customers and suppliers.

'Set up a business.'

In order to set up his own business, one man purchased items of clothing which were 'seconds' that he sold from his car boot at markets. As he made a profit, he was able to gradually purchase more stock and eventually diversified into selling 'nibbles' such as peanuts and potato chips. During the research interview he was anxious to establish that, while income had been his initial motivator, the social interaction with customers and other stall-holders was now one of the most important contributing factors to his well-being.

It is important to note that, as many new business ventures fail, you should think carefully before you commit hard-earned retirement savings.

The desire to replace work

'The more you have been vocationally involved, the harder it is to adjust to retirement.'

'I missed the challenges of work very much in the first twelve months.'

'Have a routine to differentiate weekends from weekdays, otherwise everything becomes grey.'

'Professionals want to exercise their minds. I was used to high stress—I miss stress and feel like a prisoner.'

'Keep alive intellectually. Understand the wider issues impacting on society, otherwise you relinquish your professionalism.'

'You lose the company of workmates.'

'Have things in place to replace your job.'

'I found that it is hard to handle the psychology of leaving a high stress job to do nothing.'

'Business people/teachers etc. need hobbies/interest.'

As you would imagine, there have been countless studies on what it is that motivates us to like or dislike work. The motivating factors for work are segmented into two broad categories, that is *intrinsic* motivation which relates to the work itself, and *extrinsic* motivation which refers to rewards that are external to the work. As you examine the following list of intrinsic and extrinsic motivators in the workplace, you will see that most of them are also relevant to the benefits of having purposeful activities in retirement.

Intrinsic motivators include:

◆ satisfaction gained from using a skill for which you are trained;

◆ satisfaction gained from doing a job well;

◆ satisfaction gained from the challenges presented by the task; and

◆ satisfaction gained from confirming to yourself that you are a skilled or valuable person.

Extrinsic motivators include:

◆ promotion and status;

◆ money—pay or bonuses;

◆ recognition—for example, being recognised by your peers as hard working or as skilled in a particular area;

◆ benefits/perks—for example, the use of the president's car space at your club; and

◆ access to social networks, work friends.

The desire for balance

'Balance your interests with seeing people.'

'It is vital to have a wide range of interests, otherwise I get depressed.'

'Have something to do and also have periods to do nothing.'

The need for having balance in our lives is probably best summed up by the old expression, 'The grass is always greener on the other side of the fence.' When we are at work, many of us long to be on holidays. As a long holiday draws to a close some people will say, 'I'm looking forward to getting back to work—I feel recharged now.'

The notion of balance is a recurring theme in the physical sciences, in politics, in philosophy and in psychology. Balance is also at the heart of the concept of 'everything in moderation', which those in the various health sciences typically espouse. Following are some examples of how the concept of balance occurs across a range of life situations.

Homeostasis Homeostasis is the tendency of your body to re-establish equilibrium when various components get out of balance, for example, salt levels, sugar levels, or white and red cell levels. At a psychological level, homeostasis also explains why you eventually need a break when you are overworked, or require challenges when you have been inactive for too long.

Mind versus body Does the way you think influence the way you feel, or does the way you feel influence the way you think? As medical and psychological research indicates that there is a strong relationship between the two, you need to ensure that you remain well in both areas for true health.

Nature versus nurture What influences your behaviour more, your genetic make-up or the environment in which you were raised? The debate continues to rage despite increasingly sophisticated methods of examining genetic effects, and in spite of the many studies of twins separated at birth and brought up in different environments. The answer to this question is probably a balance of the two influences.

Facilitating anxiety versus stress Most people will have heard of the term 'good stress', which refers to the need of all people to be challenged enough to stimulate interest. In psychology this stimulation is referred to as 'facilitating anxiety'. However, if anxiety levels become too high due to increased workloads or to unreasonable degrees of difficulty then you will suffer from stress and become *dis*tressed. Alternatively, if you are understimulated you will become bored and anxious. The key is a healthy balance between being challenged and participating in sufficient recreation.

Yin versus Yang Yin and Yang refers to the Chinese philosophy that describes the universe as comprising two opposing forces. The philosophy states that Yin represents the passive, or female, aspects of life which needs to be balanced with Yang, which represents the active, or male, aspects of life.

The desire for structure

'Keep a full diary to look forward to things.'

'Gear up with an initial weekly schedule.'

'Learn to live without the structure of work—take steps to keep busy.'

'Planning ahead for activities is important.'

'Have some structure in your life.'

'You need to have things you have to do to keep motivated.'

'Aim to find happiness in "daily" events rather than striving for success.'

'Have a "subject" to address each day.'

For some people, the structure provided by the workplace was a curse that restricted your freedom; for others, it provided a sense of security. Whatever you felt about work, the mad rush at breakfast time to catch the 7.04 train or to arrive at work in time for the 8.00 meeting provided you with structured activities from Monday to Friday. If you did not conform, you lost your job.

Some occupations are associated with very high levels of structure. For those retiring from the military, leaving that especially highly structured environment can be quite unnerving. One man in the research had been a very highly ranked officer in one of the armed forces. Soon after retiring, he was involved in a car accident that he attributed to his lack of driving experience after years of having a car and driver as part of his position. For other retired military personnel, the 'Friday afternoon–Monday morning' suddenness of the transition from a highly structured environment to an unstructured one was very stressful, leading in some cases to significant levels of anxiety and depression.

Like their military counterparts, men and women working in blue-collar occupations were accustomed to working in a relatively highly supervised work environment. This environment, while restrictive at one level, provided clear behavioural boundaries and a sense of security. One former blue-collar worker from a large industrial organisation recognised the importance of structure to his own sense of well-being and on retiring, imposed his own!

> 'I have set up a large metal workshop in our double garage next to the house. Each weekday I get up at the same time that I did when I was working, change into my overalls, and have breakfast. Straight after breakfast, I go to the workshop and work until lunchtime. I take an hour off for lunch that I have with my wife back in the house. After lunch I return to the workshop until I knock off at 4.00.'

Not too many people will wish to impose this level of discipline on themselves, nevertheless, apart from providing structure, the discipline this man applied to himself allowed him to continue to enjoy utilising his skills as a qualified toolmaker while making parts of cars for his friends and family, thereby saving them costly repairs.

The desire to be busy

> 'Have plenty to do.'

> 'Don't sit and watch the traffic go by.'

> 'Take up something that you really like and get stuck into it—go flat out to keep busy.'

> 'Don't vegetate—keep busy.'

> 'Don't go to seed.'

> 'Be fully occupied—put in a full day doing the things that you enjoy. Mix with people you can help and whose company you can enjoy.'

> 'It's a case of "drones" versus "actives"—drones die of boredom.'

> 'Do something. Don't stagnate—join a club.'

Everyone enjoys having challenges and being able to function as normal, intelligent human beings. Lying in a hammock on a tropical island may look ideal on a travel brochure but, as most people eventually realise, it is not active or challenging enough to keep them satisfied in the long term. You need to be busy and your first job after retiring should be to seek out clubs, activities and other interests that will keep you occupied.

The desire for fun

'Don't feel immobilised about sticking to your original plan. Being able to move on is important—have fun. Use lateral thinking—please yourself.'

'Have interesting activities.'

'Stay interested and active.'

'Try different voluntary roles until you find one that makes you happy.'

'Do what you "want" to do, not what you "have" to do.'

'I started out by joining everything, but you eventually decide to cut out all but those activities that are enjoyable.'

'To each his own re activities—you must choose a club or activity that suits you and keeps you busy.'

'Do the fun things you haven't had time for in your working life.'

'Work with a group where you like the people—if you find that they get on your goat, get out.'

Fun, like beauty, is very much in the eye of the beholder. Retired people provided two recurring views when it came to ensuring that they built fun into their lives. First, many commented that after a life working hard to pay the bills, discharge the mortgage and educate the kids it was now *their* time to lighten up and have some fun. One man who spent much of his time visiting the terminally ill also recognised the need to have activities that were light-hearted and pleasurable. In his particular case the fun gained from taking a day trip to the country gave him the opportunity to recharge his batteries so that he could continue to offer a quality service when visiting the hospital.

'I could have got stuck in a corner reading books for the blind.'

Second, people can become so determined to remain active that they overcommit or become involved in activities that they are not enjoying. One woman started out recording books for the blind soon after retiring. Without really intending to, she soon found herself recording three days per week. In the end, it was simply too much time out of her schedule and she eventually reduced the load to free herself up for other activities.

The desire for mental and physical stimulation

'Be busy mentally and physically.'

'Choose activities that are useful and that involve mental and physical work.'

'I need a hobby—something to think about.'

'Keep mentally and physically active—if you vegetate you are gone.'

'Plan to have something to do to keep active at three levels: physical, mental and spiritual. At the spiritual level it can either be religion or your personal code, your way of life—it doesn't matter.'

'Do something to keep mentally and physically active—organise activity, even if it requires training.'

'Have something to do to stimulate your intellect.'

'Keep busy—keep your body and brain working.'

'You need to prepare alternative activities that involve mental/physical stimulation and social contact.'

These people all had one goal in common: they did not wish to atrophy, and many of them were fond of using the expression 'use it or lose it'. You need to keep your mind and body functioning and vital by using them. You only have to think back to a time when you have been bedridden, even for just a few days, to gain insight into the comparative weakness that you experience from not using your muscles. After longer illnesses you may find that it also takes a while to get your mind back into gear. This situation is no different in retirement if you move from the challenges of full-time work to an inactive lifestyle.

The desire to mix with people and create social networks

'Join a club—mix with people.'

'Plan to have what you need to have around you (social networks).'

'Ensure you have something to enjoy—an interest where you meet people.'

'Keep yourself occupied—mentally and physically. Keep mixing with people.'

For most of us, purposeful activity involves contact with other people. Depending on your individual need to socialise, this may range from regular interaction through membership of committees to other activities involving contact with others. For some, social contact may just involve spasmodic contact with friends and neighbours. However, it is important for everyone to ensure that they have some contact with others at least weekly where possible—social isolation is not good for anyone.

The desire for adventure

'Leave yourself open to "unlikely suggestions", for example, running community activities.'

'Be prepared to change, be happy, do things that make you happy. Look at all the options.'

Only a few people cited the need for adventure as a desirable part of their retirement experience. One particularly adventurous person decided halfway to an Asian destination to get off the plane at the next airport and to stay in that country for six months just to 'see what it was like'. While he reportedly had a wonderful time, this type of spontaneous behaviour is certainly not for everyone.

Other people used retirement to realise lifelong dreams. One man in his 60s spent two years learning to fly a light aircraft. Once he felt he had achieved his ambition he ceased flying, now satisfied that he had achieved his goal and had survived at the same time! Less than five kilometres from this man's home in Adelaide, a similarly aged woman decided that she was going to try parachuting at least once in her life. At the time we spoke she had made five jumps and was eagerly looking forward to her next.

These examples represented some of the more dramatic activities undertaken by people to meet their needs for adventure. Other people embarked on trips around Australia, went on an overseas trip or started a business.

The desire to produce income

People who worked to produce income tended to fall into one of two categories. First, there were those who cheerfully welcomed work because of the opportunities it provided for activity and social interaction. For them, income was an important but secondary goal. In several of these instances the part-time job involved helping out in the business of an adult child, or returning to work part-time in the business they had originally established some years before. For others, it was consulting or working part-time for a local business. Many people commented that they regularly had to say no to offers of longer hours from employers delighted to find an enthusiastic and reliable worker.

Second, there were those people who were forced to work and who found this situation irksome. Some were victims of unexpected marriage break-ups in later life. In such instances, women were particularly badly affected as often their superannuation was inadequate due to their comparatively short time in the workforce, or due to their level of pay in unskilled roles. Others had to work due to the loss of a business or farm. In some cases, the business failure had also included the loss of their family home as part of the business loan guarantee.

Ways of using purposeful activities

This section lists some of the ways you can utilise purposeful activities to enrich your life.

Planning for activities before you retire

> *'Have creative interests years prior to retirement so that you don't notice the jolt. If you leave it until you retire you will be disappointed in your lack of skills.'*

> *'Before you retire, start building bridges so that you have something to do in retirement.'*

'Get involved in things you like before you retire because retirement is a shock to the system and you can lose the self-confidence to start something new. You should have a lot of things you like doing.'

'Think realistically about what to do before you retire—have a lot of things to do.'

'You should develop interests before retirement and move smoothly into them at retirement.'

'When you are still working, develop interests apart from work—then put them into action.'

'Plan your retirement—know what you are going to do during the day.'

'Make sure you have an activity/business or absorbing hobby to go into.'

'Get involved in clubs, charity—start exploring options. Subscribe to relevant publications.'

'Think about all the things you want to do. Plan—don't walk into an empty space. Do it well in advance of leaving work.'

In some parts of the world, it is common for larger organisations and government departments to offer employees the opportunity to phase down from full employment gradually so that they are not thrown into retirement overnight. Research into this concept has confirmed the benefits of allowing people to wind down progressively for a couple of years before retirement. Such schemes typically work by introducing a four-day week for some months, then a three day week for a further few months and so on. At the same time people in the pre-retirement phase of work receive counselling on how best to prepare for their lifestyle.

Unfortunately, pre-retirement schemes are not entrenched in most corporate or government work cultures. Nevertheless, a number of participants had individually approached their employers and arranged to work for three- or four-day weeks for the last year of their time with the organisation. (If you are still working and are thinking of this option be sure to check the possible negative impacts such a move will have on your superannuation retirement benefit. In some superannuation plans, a reduction in income during the last year(s) of work will significantly reduce the amount paid on retirement.) Others took it upon themselves to insure against a jolt at retirement by commencing a number of activities well before the date. By creating continuity of activities spanning pre-retirement and retirement life, these people were able to smooth the transition.

The unsuspecting computer expert

Patricia (not her real name) lives in a large city. Soon after she retired, she was approached by one of her friends who wanted to learn the basics of a computer word processing package. Her friend was compiling a family history and had found that typing and retyping pages of information was preventing her from producing a quality product.

As Patricia pondered the best way to teach a beginner the computer skills she had acquired over a number of years, an idea dawned. Surely if her friend wanted to learn about computers there would be others in a similar position. Moreover, word processing was only one computer skill that she had picked up; she was also skilled at using electronic spreadsheets and presentation packages.

Having first used her friend as a guinea pig, Patricia placed a small advertisement in the local paper. In her advertisement, Patricia explained that her courses were low cost, easy for beginners to follow and were fun to do.

Gradually the business built up as satisfied customers told their friends. Patricia was now in business and had a paying purposeful activity.

A range of activities

'Have options in case you lose physical ability.'

It is important to plan a range of activities in case of health problems, as your state of health clearly affects the type of activities in which you can participate. One woman described her intense frustration when the onset of rheumatoid arthritis forced her to give up painting quite early in retire-ment. She had previously envisaged a lifestyle in which she would fulfil her dream of painting full time and augmenting her income by selling paintings at craft markets.

A few people were so concerned about the prospect of ill-health that they developed a range of activities in case a particular body function failed due to arthritis, heart attack or stroke. Their activities included such diverse pursuits as golf and walking, computing, reading and mem-berships or management of clubs or other organisations. If a stroke or a prolonged period of illness then precluded one or more of the activities, there were still others that could be accessed.

Being 'active' in your activities

While working on committees is not a role that everyone relishes, at least consider increasing your level of participation in the clubs or organisa-tions you join. Many people reported that their enjoyment and their level of friendship with club members increased once they started making a personal contribution rather than being a passive member.

> 'Don't just go along to clubs and have others organise everything for you—the ones who do the organising are the ones who get the most out of it and enjoy it the most.'

> 'You have got to become active and involved and not just in one thing.'

Having a realistic view of activities

No doubt you have heard of job experience programs where teenagers in the final years of their secondary schooling spend some time working in an occupational setting such as an office or department store. One of the most significant learning outcomes from work experience comes from the opportunity to compare the realities of day-to-day work life with one's perceptions of the role.

For some students, work experience confirms that they are on the right track and should continue their plans to undertake study to quali-fy as an architect or as a teacher. For others, the experience is a rude awakening when they may learn that life as a corporate lawyer is nothing like that portrayed in their favourite TV show.

Unfortunately, in Australia few 'retirement experience' programs are available to allow us to experience life in retirement before the actual event! However, issues concerning unrealistic perceptions of retirement are just as common as those of young people seeking information regarding a career.

> *'I used to love playing in the jazz band one night a week at the pub, and dreamed of the day when I could play on all the day gigs too. I soon learned that day work for a full-time jazz musician involves engagements such as playing in ghastly shopping centres. Here members of the band may find themselves traipsing up and down escalators following luminaries like Father Christmas or the Easter Bunny to promote a store sale.'*

> *'I was going to sit in the sun and read books but I haven't had time.'*

These comments confirm that perceptions of retirement are not always congruent with reality. People regularly mentioned that the laid back lifestyle they had expected turned out to be busy and fulfilling, with spare time being as scarce as when they were working.

Motivating yourself

> *'You may have to force yourself to be active—but then it is rewarding.'*

> *'One shouldn't wait for things to happen—get involved in things, for example, consultancies, activities for the mind, get involved in the community.'*

> *'Don't sit around and be lonely—become involved.'*

> *'You need to have interesting things to do—but you still need incentive.'*

> *'A lot of retirees go into their shell and don't want to participate.'*

> *'Keep motivated. Keep interested (turn off the TV)—keep learning.'*

> *'Don't give up—look for something you like to do.'*

> *'Don't sit on your backside—go out and make it happen.'*

> *'You've got to be ready and mentally prepared to have activities. If you can also earn from them, fine!'*

> *'Make yourself join clubs/groups.'*

'Look at what your friends do and get ideas—keep busy, otherwise you dwell on problems.'

Some people are naturally well organised and put their ideas into action quickly after conceiving them. There are those who are so extraverted that their high need for contact with people automatically drives them to seek social activities on a regular basis. For many people, however, it takes real effort to join new clubs or organisations, or to push themselves to investigate potential activities. Where people are having trouble getting started in new activities, particularly where it involves joining in with groups of people, it may be due to one or more of the following reasons:

◆ **They are not sure what is expected of them and may feel nervous about starting at the new club or activity.** Do some research. Find out what people wear there, what is expected of members and how formal or informal the meetings are. This will help you relax when you realise that you will fit in after all!

◆ **They feel they will be inadequate and will be rejected by others.** Do more research. Try to find out whether the activity is one you see yourself enjoying. Will the people there be good company for you? Are they the type of people you like mixing with?

◆ **They are concerned that the benefits to be gained from participating may be outweighed by the personal efforts/costs required.** Ask yourself if this is just an excuse to put off making an effort. Are you just trying to take the easy way out?'

The impact of aging on purposeful activities

'People need to think of the impact of aging on their lifestyle in retirement. I started an orchard but didn't think through how much physical hard work would be involved. You need therefore to get advice on what to expect—not just today but down the track when you are older.'

Only a few of the people raised the issue of aging with relation to their decision to establish a purposeful activity. Yet the relevance of aging is significant, particularly where capital is invested in an income-producing activity. The man quoted purchased a property with the intention of setting up a fruit orchard. He had done all the right things such as conducting market research and learning to run a profitable farm and had identified the specific agricultural issues pertinent to growing fruit. He was soon running a successful business. His problem centred on the fact that much of the hard work of harvesting and pruning came years later when the orchard was established. By then he was older and was beginning to suffer from arthritis, which hampered his ability to perform some tasks around the farm. Had he known the level of hard physical work, and the fact that he was going to develop arthritis, he probably would still have pursued his dream. However, more informed planning would have enabled him to prepare better for the time when he would need to delegate some work around the farm to others.

Avoiding destructive activities

'Don't get involved in destructive activities, for example, playing poker machines.'

The financial effects of the introduction of poker machines in Victoria horrified one woman, who spoke of people she knew who had lost most of their life savings and, in one case, their home. She believed that many of these people were simply lonely and that the enticing environment of the gaming rooms conspired to give them a misguided sense of purpose and belonging.

Excessive alcohol consumption was also a problem for some people, particularly those who lived alone. Again, while some would have certainly been suffering from alcoholism before retirement, many heavy drinkers claimed they overindulged due to the boredom brought on by a lack of meaningful activities.

Sources of purposeful activities

The range of potential activities is limited only by your imagination; here are a few ideas to help you get the ball rolling.

Speak with other people who have retired. Ask others what they do with their time in retirement. Keep asking—don't just stop after you have spoken to one or two people. Eventually you will find someone who has an activity that appeals to you.

Form a purposeful activities task force. If you have friends for whom finding a suitable activity is also an issue, set up a task force. Hold regular meetings over a cup of coffee and generate ideas together for things to do. During the meeting, set everyone the task of seeking out five people with whom they will discuss suggested activities. Reconvene the meeting in a fortnight and have everyone report on their findings. Warn everyone in advance to be positive and to persist so that no one has any excuses for coming back without some ideas.

Your local library Visit your local library and check the noticeboard for any clubs or activities that may be listed there. Ask the librarian for any ideas or local contacts they may have.

Your local community office Most local communities produce a booklet once a year that lists the activities and organisations in your area. Also, get hold of the booklets from your neighbouring communities, which may have groups that are close enough to be accessed. The reason for looking wider than your own community is that some are better than others; if your own community is a little impoverished for contacts, the others nearby may be better.

Your local papers Notices and articles about coming events are often reported in the local newspaper. For example, you may find an article about a club or association that you find interesting. Papers are also a good way of keeping in touch with issues affecting your immediate community.

The Yellow Pages Think of some activity you are interested in and you will often be able to find a club or organisation that fosters its interests. Checking the Yellow Pages under 'Clubs' is a good place to start.

Short courses Adult education and night classes run in most areas. Contact your local colleges/libraries or the Department of Education for information.

Voluntary work Many organisations will be grateful for your help. If you wish to donate your services try the local charities, churches, or hospitals as a starting point. The type of help you provide can be direct to those in need, for example delivering meals-on-wheels, or indirect such as helping on fund-raising committees of service organisations such as Lions or Rotary.

Form an interest group Some people start their own interest groups and these do not have to be large or difficult to arrange. For example, if you are interested in the Internet, you could find a couple of friends with similar interests and meet once a month to discuss the latest sites. Those friends could then invite other friends and the group would grow as you desired.

The Internet If you are connected to the Internet, you will already be aware of the enormous number of web-based groups across the world that are set up for people with the most obscure to the most popular interests. To use the Internet at home, you need to:

◆ have the telephone connected;

◆ have a suitable computer;

◆ have a modem (which connects your computer to the Internet via your phone line); and

◆ join an Internet Service Provider (ISP), who provides the necessary software and for a fee connects you to the Internet. ISPs can be found in the Yellow Pages.

It is also a good idea to speak to a couple of friends who are connected to the Internet and get their advice regarding the quality of their ISP, pricing etc.

Most local libraries have an Internet terminal and will introduce you to the concept so that you can judge whether you wish to commit to purchasing the resources to have your own Internet connection at home. Once you are connected, you can also use e-mail (electronic mail) to make contact with other people all over the world.

Case study—Fay and Ron

When it comes to ensuring that they are involved in purposeful activities, Fay and Ron set a cracking pace. Their range of pastimes is as diverse as their commitment is substantial.

Fay is a retired bookkeeper; her activities include the following:

- Secretary of a local club, where she also attends to the mailing and agendas for club meetings: 2 hours per week.

- Committee member for a local nursing home, where she also helps organise their fund-raising fetes: 2 hours per week.

- Visits to her mother each evening in the nursing home to feed her and provide company. On the weekends she also visits at lunchtimes: 8 hours per week.

- She is a beauty therapist and runs her own business: 20 hours per week.

- She is an experienced dressmaker. Sometimes this involves a small amount of time per week; on other occasions, Fay has been known to work into the small hours of the morning to finish off a wedding gown and bridesmaids' dresses: varies.

- She is the secretary of the local jazz club, attending to the minutes, agendas, correspondence and a food platter for the band at the monthly club functions: 2 hours per week.

In addition to these activities, Fay maintains the home for herself, her husband Ron and their adult daughter. Fay tries to take Tuesdays off, but not surprisingly does not always succeed in meeting this goal!

Ron is a retired corporate secretary and qualified accountant. His activities include the following:

- Newsletter editor for the local jazz club. Ron writes the newsletter editorial and arranges for the preparation and mail of the newsletter to members: 5 hours per week.

- Chairman of the local management accounting group, where he also arranges speakers and venues for their meetings: 2 hours per month.

- He subcontracts to a superannuation auditor: 4–5 hours per week.

- He runs his own growing finance brokerage, office services and accounting packages supply and installation business: 5.5 days per week.

- He is treasurer for a state branch of the Australian Republican Movement: 8 hours per month.

- He lectures in accounting and computing (night classes): 3–4 hours per week.

- He has conducted budgeting courses for real estate agents: varies.

- He conducts telemarketing campaigns for his finance business: during the day in the office.

- He tries to find time for at least one game of bowls and one game of golf per week: varies.
- He is a member of the Fellowship of Australian Writers and writes poetry in his spare time: varies.

In addition to the above, Ron maintains their garden.

Ron and Fay also plan for a two-week holiday every two years, visiting overseas islands.

CHECKLIST

❑ I have checked the booklet produced by my municipal council, and the booklets of neighbouring councils, for the clubs and associations near my area.

❑ I have asked relatives and friends for ideas about activities and will continue to seek ideas from people that I meet.

❑ I have contacted my local library for information, ideas and contacts for clubs, associations, charity work etc.

❑ I have contacted local churches and charities for ideas regarding activities, groups to join, volunteer work required etc.

❑ I have thought about crafts, hobbies, trades or topics for study that I am interested in, and will explore activities centred around these.

❑ I have explored the possibility of voluntary work with organisations such as the St Vincent de Paul Society, the Red Cross, my local hospital etc.

❑ I regularly check the daily and local papers for ideas and information about clubs and interest groups in my neighbourhood.

❑ I have checked the 'Clubs' listing of the Yellow Pages for ideas.

❑ I have thought about starting my own interest group or club.

SECTION II:

Maintaining and managing relationships

Maintaining effective and mutually supportive relationships with partners, adult children and friends is important to our sense of well-being at any time in our lives. Once you have retired, the need for social interaction is further heightened by the fact that overnight you find yourself removed from the social network previously provided by the workplace. At this time, retirement can also bring stresses due to the natural adjustment process that accompanies any significant life change.

Relationships are particularly important because being able to share with others what you are feeling and how you are coping is an important factor in successful adjustment to your new lifestyle. You also have a responsibility to 'be there' for your friends and relatives who may be experiencing their own dilemmas as they adjust to retirement.

Through the experiences of the 200 people who participated in the *Retire 200* research program, you will learn how the relationships of others were affected during retirement. Five key areas of relationship management are discussed.

First, the important issue of communication within relationships is examined. What is happening when communication fails is identified and simple steps to improve it are provided.

Second, you will be shown how to use simply applied assertiveness skills to maximise opportunities for obtaining your rights with a minimum of stress.

Third, it will be shown how to handle the difficulties that can arise when conflict occurs between friends or neighbours. The best ways to negotiate with business people when purchasing goods or services are also examined.

Fourth, ways in which you can nurture and maintain close relationships with your partner and others are examined.

Fifth, the importance of contributing and belonging once you have retired is looked at. With the social networks formerly provided by the workplace now severed, it becomes even more important for you to remain connected to your family and community.

These insights will help you to improve aspects of your relationships that are presently not as satisfying as you would like them to be.

Chapter 2

Communicating effectively within relationships

The aims of this chapter are to:

◆ examine the importance of maintaining effective communication in relationships;

◆ learn new skills for improving the effectiveness of your communication style;

◆ learn how to apply powerful listening skills; and

◆ learn how to manage the poor communication styles of others.

The effects of poor communication within relationships

Everyone has experienced how tense they become when, due to poor communication, things go wrong in their relationships. At least when you were in the workplace you had the opportunity to allow an argument at home to dissipate as you threw yourself into your work. Being separated during the day also allowed both the time and emotional space to cool off from an argument and to perhaps even start composing an apology (even if it was almost certainly the other partner's fault!). Once you have both retired, however, it is not as easy to 'escape' from each other, particularly if one of your post-retirement financial decisions has been to retain only one car that you share.

'We rarely talk to each other these days. If you are not happy, then retirement won't cure it. Therefore, get your relationship fixed up and get your priorities right.'

After years of being apart during the day, couples suddenly find themselves interacting at a personal level on just about everything they do. Consequently, those who have a solid relationship based on mutual respect and open communication will fare better than those for whom trust, respect and communication are impoverished. One man found that retirement placed insurmountable pressures on his already fragile relationship with his wife and, sadly, they parted soon after. Other couples discovered that, even where their basic relationship was sound, communication could still break down under the special pressures brought about by retirement.

Being seen to communicate

There is an old saying that states, 'Justice must not only be done—it must be seen to be done.' Similar sentiments apply to the communication processes between partners and friends. As often as not, the real issue is not so much *what* is being said, but *how* it is being conveyed. Communication involves more than just two people alternatively speaking and listening; effective communication also involves the process of 'active listening'. When you listen actively you do not just hear, but are seen to be hearing by the way in which you physically and mentally attend to the other person.

Mary *(hearing Steve arrive home):* 'Steve, guess what!'

Steve *(just noticing a bill on the table):* 'Uh! What?'

Mary: 'I was elected president of the club today!'

Steve *(now horrified as he reads the 'bottom line' of the bill):* 'Uh! Oh! Good.'

Mary *(exasperated as she notes his distraction):* 'You haven't heard a thing I've just said!'

Steve: *'Yes I did! You've just been made president of the club.'*

Did that type of exchange sound familiar? Steve 'heard' what Mary said. However, from Mary's perspective, their communication was not satisfying—he just was not 'listening'. How many times have you been the victim or perpetrator of this type of impoverished communication? How did you feel when you were on the receiving end?

Sharing decision-making

'... I don't know why he didn't consult me on his choice of superannuation fund—he can't even balance his own cheque book! Now I find we've been locked into a low performing portfolio for twenty years.'

Financial problems can be a major source of relationship strain at *any* time of life, however, in retirement this is particularly true where finances are usually limited to a fixed income. It is therefore important that partners discuss any financial plans and decisions that are going to significantly affect their lifestyle. When one-sided financial decisions impact negatively on retirement income, stress resulting from arguments over money is bound to occur. Just as important is the damage caused to the relationship when one person feels devalued by their partner's poor consultation and the implicit lack of trust in their judgment. Even in relationships where one partner looks after the finances, it is still important to at least discuss what transactions are taking place and how they will affect living standards.

Improving communication in your relationships

Communicating support for your partner's interests

'She is always complaining about me "wasting time mucking around in that stupid workshop". What she doesn't understand is that since I have retired this hobby has become very important to my sanity—I need to be doing something.'

The changed circumstances created by retirement often increase the relevance of existing hobbies or interests. What was once a hobby involving a couple of hours here and there on a Saturday afternoon may become a daily activity replacing much of the sense of purpose and interest previously provided by the workplace. Yet a common complaint occurred where people failed to understand the importance of the activity to their partner, a situation that caused unnecessary anxiety when they were made to feel guilty for wasting time or money on their pastime or interest.

The three most common reasons given for failing to recognise a partner's need to pursue their hobby were:

◆ where the hobby or pastime was perceived by the other partner to lack a practical outcome, such as income from the sale of items produced in a workshop;

◆ where financial resources were directed to the hobby at the expense of other 'priorities'; and

◆ where the person looking on suspected that their partner was primarily involved in the activity as a way of escaping from them!

If your partner resents the time you are spending on your pastime, you need to think carefully about how you are going to communicate to them why your activity is important to you. If you suspect that you are going to have difficulty with this communication, you may wish to consider the following points when explaining the importance of your pastime to your partner:

'It replaces some of the structure to my day previously provided by work.'

'It provides me with one more reason to get up in the morning and feel enthusiastic.'

'Involvement in pastimes is my way of remaining mentally alert and physically fit.'

'Activity meets my need to be busy due to my work ethic.'

'My activity is fun! I enjoy it!'

Maximising effective communication in relationships

There are two aspects of communication that are at the heart of most so-called 'communication breakdowns'. First, the *content* of what is being communicated is not fully understood by the receiver. Poor communication of this type can be due to a number of reasons such as:

◆ the listener's lack of trust or respect for the speaker;

◆ the listener's preconceived view of what the speaker really means; or

◆ not listening attentively due to lack of interest in the topic.

Second, but just as important, is the *style* or tone of interpersonal communication you use. Interestingly, the closer you are to someone, the more dysfunctional your chosen communication style may be! Using poor styles such as talking down to your partner can result in resentment and anger that can seriously damage a relationship. It is therefore important that you get it right.

The following sections look at the skills you need to use to com-municate accurately and effectively with your partner and friends.

Listening—the hardest part of effective communication

Let me warn you now! If you become skilled in this difficult aspect of communicating, you may find that people who want to pour out their hearts will regularly besiege you! Genuine 'active listening', the type that psychologists are paid for, is easy to describe, easy to understand in theory, but exhaustingly difficult to put into practice.

The reason that effective communication can be so demanding is that it involves the use of a number of communication skills at once. As these skills do not usually come naturally to most people, they take considerable practice to master. However, if you are determined to put in the work on your interpersonal communication skills you *will* see results.

Notwithstanding the hard work associated with learning and applying effective communication skills, there are times in every relationship where it is of the utmost importance to both listen and to be heard. To further complicate matters, it is sometimes important to communicate most effectively at the very time when effective communication is at its most difficult to achieve! An example could be where there is an emotional issue affecting you both, such as the unexpected terminal illness of a close mutual friend. Remaining calm and objectively discussing how you can both assist your friend will be more difficult if you have trouble communicating under normal circumstances.

How to listen 'actively'

Remember how Mary reacted to Steve when he read the bill while she was trying to celebrate her good news? How many times have *you* heard someone say, 'You are not listening to me!' Were you doing something else while the person was speaking, such as fiddling with something, daydreaming, or were you just conveying the impression that you were bored? The process of 'active listening' vastly improves such poor communication.

The acronym S-O-L-E-R is sometimes used to describe the high level of active listening skills used in counselling. Effective communication involves the listener attending to each of five processes. If you become skilled in these communication skills you will find that you, and those with whom you are communicating, will benefit enormously.

Face the person Squarely: Have you noticed how pleasant it is when someone you are talking to turns towards you to listen? You feel as if they are absorbing and valuing what you say. On the other hand, we have all experienced situations where a bored shop assistant takes your food order while they grumpily wipe down a counter. It does not leave you with much confidence that you will get what you ordered, does it!

Use an Open posture: There is no need to be fanatical about this step. For example, it is quite okay to sit with your legs crossed if this is more comfortable. However, folding your arms across your chest should be avoided as this behaviour may be interpreted as being judgmental or defensive.

Lean towards the person: Leaning forward a little indicates to the other person that you are interested in what they are saying. You will notice people who are discussing an interesting topic sometimes lean forward as they become animated, which may be where the saying, 'I was sitting on the edge of my seat!' comes from. On the other hand, getting very comfortable and sliding down in your chair in a reclining or slouching manner can indicate that you are more interested in your own comfort than in what the other person is saying.

Maintain appropriate Eye contact: Maintaining appropriate eye contact indicates to the other person that you are attending to them. This does not mean fixing them with an unrelenting, steely eyed stare, but rather maintaining regular eye contact. Gazing out the window or picking at a loose thread on your clothing indicates pretty clearly that you are not focusing on what they are saying.

Relax: Before you start the communication process, think about how you are presenting yourself. Are you acting tensely, or indicating that you do not approve of the person? If so, communication will certainly break down—you need to get yourself reasonably relaxed.

If the SOLER skills are to become an effective part of your communication repertoire, you will need to practise them and then use them regularly.

'Listening to' non-verbal language (body language)

There has been a lot of nonsense written about 'body language' in pop psychology books. Some people would have you believe that you can read a person's mind simply by watching how they sit, whether they scratch the left side of their nose or the right, and so on. This is not to say that body language, or non-verbal language as it is correctly termed, does not provide valuable insights into what a person is communicating when they speak. The real key to interpreting non-verbal behaviour is to look at the context in which it appears. For example, if I sit down and fold my arms it could be for any one of the following reasons:

- ◆ I have just come in from a blustering winter's wind and I am cold.

- ◆ I may be feeling defensive and threatened by the topic being discussed.

- ◆ I may have a pain in my back that is relieved by sitting with my arms folded.

- ◆ I may be trying to hide the mayonnaise stain on my tie.

An example of interpreting non-verbal language in context could be where I am sitting in an open posture and then suddenly fold my arms if someone accuses me of doing something unpleasant. Here it is reasonable to suspect that I am feeling defensive (but not necessarily guilty!).

Non-verbal behaviour should also be congruent with and should confirm what is being said. For example, if I were to say, 'I've never felt so happy and carefree' while frowning sternly, you would need to ask more questions to see which one of the conflicting messages was correct!

Listening to verbal language

When people communicate with you they will do so at three levels:

1. **Their experiences:** The person you are communicating with will tell you *what* is happening that is affecting their lives. 'Last night I heard a loud noise in the backyard.'

2. **Their behaviours:** The person you are communicating with will tell you about their *actions/behaviours*. 'I got out of bed as quietly as I could and peeped through the curtains to see if I could make out what had made the noise.'

3. **Their feelings:** The person you are communicating with will tell you how they are *feeling* either physically and/or emotionally. 'My heart was pounding and I felt very scared.'

While you will find that people will frequently tell you *what* happened to them (Experiences), and *how* they reacted (Behaviours), they frequently leave it to you to gauge how they *felt* because to them it appears so obvious. An experienced counsellor realises at this point that it is important to seek clarification by saying something like,

'How did you feel about that?' or 'Were you very upset?'

Further questions can then be used to identify what it was about the event that caused them the most anguish. The following example demonstrates a number of possible reactions to the same event.

'Yesterday, I tripped over in the city. As I fell, I tore my new trousers. A group of teenage boys on skateboards just looked at me and laughed while I lay there stunned. Eventually a young couple helped me up. I was so upset that I came straight back home without doing any shopping. I felt awful!'

Some possible reasons for your friend/partner being upset include:

◆ The trousers were new and cost a lot of money.

◆ They found being laughed at embarrassing.

◆ They were concerned by the callous behaviour of the young skateboarders and the possible implications of where society was headed.

◆ It was frightening to consider that they may have broken a bone or hip.

◆ They may have lost some confidence and were now fearful of falling again.

Depending on your own perspective you could easily jump to a number of conclusions as to why the person was upset, but by applying your own values you may be way off target. The only way you can find out what *really* upset them is to ask questions.

Making people feel 'listened to'

When a skilled professional is listening to you they will use a number of methods to signal to you that they are both hearing and understanding what you are saying. The following are a few of the techniques they use which you can put into action.

1. Gestures: Nodding and gesturing with your hand for the person to continue talking while you remain silent indicates that you are focusing on what they are saying, and that you wish them to continue without interruption from yourself.

2. Minimal encouragers: Verbal responses such as 'Mm-hm' and 'Uh-huh' are known as minimal encouragers. They motivate the person to continue talking yet contain no judgmental message that could stop the communication flow. When people are upset or embarrassed, even comparatively innocent phrases such as 'I see' may be interpreted as a negative judgment on what the person is saying, for example,

'Then I'm afraid I lost my temper and threw a glass at him.'

'Uh-huh' (rather than 'I see!')

3. Asking for clarification: When someone is upset, they may be talking to you through tears, or in a confused state of mind. If you are finding it hard to follow what they are saying, or if you have temporarily lost concentration, always seek clarification. It will demonstrate to them that you care about understanding them properly and will also reduce the likelihood of you misinterpreting the content, for example:

'I don't quite understand—what did he do after you threw the glass at him?'

4. Paraphrasing: Paraphrasing, that is, repeating back what someone has said to you using your own words, is an extremely powerful way of demonstrating that you are listening attentively. It also verifies whether you have correctly understood the meaning behind what they have said. If you find that you have misunderstood the content of their message, they will usually tell you quickly!

'After I threw the glass at him I broke down and cried.'

'So when you threw the glass you felt silly?'

'No! I felt angry and hurt!'

5. Accenting key phrases: When people are relating the details of an event or feeling that is affecting them, they may do so in a jumble of words and sentences that are disjointed and distorted by sobs as they relive the experience. It is important that you let them do most of the talking so that they can get it all out. An effective way of letting them know you are following the important parts of their message is to echo the key words or phrases that you believe are at the core of their communication:

'Then he walked out and said that he was never coming back.'

'Never coming back?'

'That's right! I couldn't believe that I was hearing it!'

Managing poor communication styles

'My husband can be so overbearing at times. I ordered some sandwiches for us in the coffee shop the other day. When they arrived, he dressed me down in front of the waitress for not asking for wholemeal bread! I felt like a child.'

Back in 1961 Dr Eric Berne wrote a book called *Transactional Analysis in Psychotherapy*, the forerunner to his successful book *The Games People Play*. In a similar vein, Dr Thomas Harris's book *I'm OK—You're OK* followed a short time later.

For a while, transactional analysis or 'TA' was all the rage in psychiatric and psychological settings. It was taught in counselling classes around the world and teachers learned its fundamentals in post-graduate teacher training courses. At an organisational level, TA became the subject of courses run by human resources consultants. Like many ideas that become popular, it was eventually viewed as a fad and later fell out of fashion in mainstream psychology.

However, when it comes to identifying poor communication styles, TA remains a relatively easy concept for people without formal counselling training to apply. It enables the quick recognition of inappropriate communication styles and, just as importantly, it provides a structure for dealing with annoying communication styles where *you* are on the receiving end.

Transactional Analysis (TA) explained

According to TA, people are described as using one of three modes of communication, namely, Parent (P), Adult (A), or Child (C). TA practitioners argue that effective communication most often occurs when we are using the Adult mode. So how do the modes differ?

Parent mode (judgmental, interfering)

When we are communicating in Parent mode, we may use the following verbal and non-verbal (body language) styles.

The way 'Parents' look	The way 'Parents' speak
Arms folded	'Now look here!'
Hands on the hips	'If I were you I would ...'
Frowning (for impact)	'Why are you always so late! Now we are going to keep Jenny waiting.'
Sighing with exasperation	'Don't ask questions—just do it!'

Are you ever on the receiving end of this type of communication? Stop and reflect for a moment about occasions when you have experienced the Parent communication style. How does it make you feel? Do you ever dish out this type of communication to others? In what sort of settings are you likely to do this?

Child mode (childish, immature)

When we are communicating in Child mode, we may use the following verbal and non-verbal (body language) styles.

The way the 'Child' looks	The way the 'Child' speaks
Tears	'I wish, I want ...'
Shrugging	Overuse of superlatives—that is, the 'mine-is-better' game
Whining	'Gee, do I have to?'
Displays of bad temper, sulking	'I don't care.'

Do you ever behave in this way? Most people do! Under what circumstances are you likely to do this?

Adult mode (mature, intelligent)

When we are communicating in Adult mode, we use the following verbal and non-verbal (body language) styles.

The way the 'Adult' looks	The way the 'Adult' speaks
Facial and body movements indicate non-judgmental listening	'Who? What? Where? When? How?'
Calm—concentrating on the interaction	'I think that is right . . .' 'In my opinion . . .'

How often do people treat you like an adult during communication? Stop and reflect for a moment on some examples that you have experienced. How does this style of communication make you feel?

The following are some examples of combinations of Parent, Child and Adult interactions:

Child–Parent interaction

Husband to wife: 'Let me watch the football, you know how much I love it. I'll cut the grass tomorrow.' (Child)

Parent-Child interaction

Wife to husband: 'Go and cut the grass first then you can watch all the TV you like.' (Parent)

Do these styles of interactions sound familiar? They are generally not satisfying for either party.

Parent–parent interactions

Sue to Jane: 'Mary looks ridiculous in that short dress—she's no spring chicken.' (Parent)

Jane to Sue: 'Oh, she is always wearing outfits like that! She's no super model.' (Parent)

Child-child interactions

John to Mary:	'I want to get that new TV—I've got to have it!' (Child)
Mary to John:	'But I want to buy that ring I showed you the other day.' (Child)

Adult-Adult interactions

Husband to wife:	'I think I will watch the football now.'
Wife to husband:	'When do you plan to cut the grass? It's getting pretty long.'

So what does all this mean? How can you use this information to improve communication in your own relationships? Essentially, when people respond in Child or Parent modes, they are attempting to get their own way in an emotionally laden and unintelligent way. For example, imagine that you needed to take an afternoon off from your rostered shift at your service club's fund-raising fete to attend to an important personal matter. You go into the club president and the conversation goes like this:

'Ian, I have an important personal matter to attend to next Saturday afternoon. Do you mind if I excuse myself from the fete that afternoon?' *(Adult)*

'Look Mary, there is no way that you can pull out now. Your role in the club is to help us meet our funding requirements — I can't have you mucking us around at this late date.' (Parent)

Nobody was satisfied here. Mary felt humiliated and resentful because her needs were ignored. Her club president, Ian, may also reflect later that he could have handled the situation better. From his point of view, it was hardly good presidential behaviour.

So what do you do when you are confronted with a response like that? For many people, their first response is to fire back an answer in either Child or Parent mode:

'Ian, I have an important personal matter to attend to next Saturday afternoon. Do you mind if I excuse myself from the fete that afternoon?' *(Adult)*

'Look Mary, there is no way that you can pull out now. Your role in the club is to help us meet our funding requirements — I can't have you mucking us around at this late date.' (Parent)

'Oh! Go on Ian! You know what a good girl I am and how hard I always work for you!' (Child)

Interestingly, this just may work! However, how satisfying is it for Mary? Do you think she would then feel valued as a mature, intelligent woman? Is this the way an enlightened club president should encourage members to act?

Here is an example of Mary responding to Ian in Parent mode:

'Ian, I have an important personal matter to attend to next Saturday afternoon. Do you mind if I excuse myself from the fete that afternoon?' (Adult)

'Look Mary, there is no way that you can pull out now. Your role in the club is to help us meet our funding requirements — I can't have you mucking us around at this late date.' (Parent)

'Look, you may be the club president but that is no way to treat people — how dare you be so inconsiderate.' (Parent)

Responding to the communication of others with Parent mode communication is how disputes often start. Such communication might make you feel good at the time but it achieves nothing until someone backs off.

What is the solution?

The ideal way to respond to the demanding Parent or the whining Child is to use the Adult mode. You may find that the other person continues in their Parent or Child mode for a time. However, if you ignore this behaviour and persist in using the Adult mode, you will increase your chances of establishing effective communication. Here is an example using Mary and Ian again.

'Ian, I have an important personal matter to attend to next Saturday afternoon. Do you mind if I excuse myself from the fete that afternoon?' (Adult)

'Look Mary, there is no way that you can pull out now. Your role in the club is

to help us meet our funding requirements — I can't have you mucking us around at this late date.' (Parent)

'Yes Ian—I realise we are busy but I do need the time off.' (Adult)

'Give me a break Mary—you don't want me to miss my fund-raising target do you?' (Child)

'Ian, it is very important that I take the time off on Saturday. Can we discuss a way for me to make up the time, say by finding a replacement to do my roster? (Adult)

'Well okay, if you can find someone reliable and who will do the job well we would still meet our objectives.' (Adult)

OR

'Mary, we have to meet our fund raising target and I am afraid that people are stretched as it is. It is just not possible to give you time off this week. Perhaps there is a way for you to change your Saturday appointment?' (Adult)

As you can see, you may not always get your way. However, the communication is effective and everyone concerned is treated like an adult of intelligence and substance. Mary held her ground by being assertive and maintaining an Adult communication mode, and her club president finally 'grew up' and behaved accordingly.

Using the Adult mode improves communication for these two important reasons:

◆ If you persist in using the Adult mode in the face of the whining Child or the overbearing Parent you will hear yourself speaking as a reasonable and intelligent person. This does wonders for your self-esteem.

◆ The annoying behaviour of the other person is eventually more likely to diminish as they hear themselves responding in an inappropriate way when compared to your reasonable, mature communication style.

Attitudinal impediments to communication

We have so far examined communication skills and how to manage dysfunctional communication styles. However, it does not matter how skilled you are if your attitude is not right. Listed below are five attitudinal issues to consider before starting effective communication.

How you are feeling

If you are not feeling well, or are presently anxious due to your own personal concerns, you may not be able to provide the high levels of energy needed to communicate effectively. If this is the case, you should let the person you are communicating with know your situation. Suggest to them that you meet with them later so that you can give them your full attention and assistance.

Their issue = your issue

The topic they may be wishing to discuss may also be a highly charged issue for you. For example, if your friend is upset because a newspaper article has brought back sad or disturbing memories, and you also find that the article triggers similar emotions in yourself, then you should point this out early in the conversation.

Enthusiasm

When people are anxious to help or to please, they may only hear half of what the other person is saying and leap in assuming they know how the person was going to complete their sentence. It is not helpful to do this because, firstly, if you get it wrong you will annoy the other person because they will then have to start their story all over again. This may be distressing for them if the topic under discussion is affecting them strongly. Secondly, even if you are correct, you are denying them the opportunity to talk matters over and to get the issues off their chest.

Preoccupation with your own problems

It is very difficult to attend to another person's problems when there is something bothering you. For example, if you were waiting for a pathology report that will determine whether you have a serious illness, then it is very difficult to empathise with someone who is complaining about a bad cold.

Defensive listening

Think back to a time when you have had to tell someone something that you knew would annoy or anger them. For example, imagine that you and your partner bought a new car six weeks ago. Today, on your way home from lunch with a friend, you scraped the side of the car as you pulled out of a tight parking space. This is the second time in twelve months that you have had such an accident and you suspect that your partner feels that the first accident was due to your carelessness. As you drive home and contemplate the conversation to come you may feel yourself becoming defensive. You 'know' what they are going to say!

Unfortunately, defensiveness is one of the most common impediments to effective communication. Just as a safe environment, where there is approval and acceptance, will encourage us to continue talking, so a negative, judgmental, evaluative environment blocks effective communication. Therefore, to help keep your own communication open and honest when you believe someone may be feeling defensive about a topic, try the following steps.

1. Be positive to the person. Try to separate your reaction to the *content* of what the person is saying from your reaction to them as a person. For instance, in the case of the scratched car, it would be helpful if the partner listening to the story said something like:

'This is very annoying—you must be upset.'

By saying this, the message conveyed is:

'I am annoyed that the car is damaged, but I am not annoyed with you.'

It also acknowledges your empathy for their feelings and embarrassment.

2. Wait before you evaluate. If you are finding the content of someone's communication annoying, it can be tempting to cut them off or to leap in with a sarcastic remark, for example:

'Where did you think you were driving—in the Grand Prix?'

It is wiser to hold back before you evaluate and let the other person get their story out in an atmosphere of trust and mutual respect. Wait until you have heard the *complete* story (and until you have calmed down if this is relevant) before making any premature or damning comments.

In other words, create the type of environment *you* would want if the boot were on the other foot!

3. Minimise your negative evaluations and feelings. As the other person is relating the story, try to minimise any tendency to tune in selectively to the negative, punitive aspects of the event. You might find yourself imagining your partner driving in a careless or erratic manner when in fact nothing may be further from the truth.

4. Encourage the person to continue even if you are becoming annoyed. Encourage the other person to speak freely and openly. If you find yourself getting upset, breathe deeply and slowly. It is probably much harder for them to discuss the topic than it is for you to listen.

Love, familiarity and intimacy—blocks to communication!

It sounds crazy, doesn't it! How can intimacy be an obstacle to effective communication? Yet a common trap that people in close relationships fall into is relying on the romantic notion that because they are in love, communication does not need to be worked at. Consequently, partners will operate on the flawed premise that 'He/she ought to know how I feel on this subject' and leave the hard work of effective communication to chance. It seems that most people have two sets of rules when it comes to interpersonal communication: one for their spouse or partner and the other for everyone else!

CHECKLIST

❑ I will try not to communicate as an overbearing 'Parent' or as a whining 'Child'.

❑ I will attend to the communications of others by using appropriate non-verbal (body language) communication to support my verbal responses.

❑ I will work hard to create an environment where open and effective communication is encouraged.

❑ I will try not to react defensively to criticism or bad news.

Chapter 3

Assertiveness skills—getting your rights without stress

The aims of this chapter are to:

◆ discuss the need for assertiveness skills in retirement;

◆ understand how assertive, non-assertive and aggressive behaviours differ; and

◆ describe how to use assertive behaviour to achieve your rights without causing yourself unnecessary stress.

What is assertiveness?

What do you think of when you hear the word 'assertive'? Do you picture someone pushing and shoving their way to the top of a queue? Do you imagine a shopper barking commands at a shop assistant? In fact, both of these situations are examples of 'aggression', where the person involved gets their way at the expense of someone else's rights or feelings. At the other end of the scale but just as ineffective is non-assertive behaviour, whereby you give up your rights out of fear or lack of confidence.

Assertiveness, on the other hand, is the calm, reasonable process of establishing and then requesting what is rightfully yours. Such rights may range from fair and equitable treatment in a relationship to the respect and service you deserve from the staff of your bank, irrespective of the size of your account balance!

To demonstrate how aggressive, non-assertive and assertive behaviours differ in style, let us say that your cousin has heard that you have a new camera and asks to borrow it during his annual holiday interstate. You have paid a lot of money for the camera and you do not wish to lend it to anyone. What is more, your cousin has a poor record when it comes to looking after other people's property. You could respond in one of three ways:

- **Aggressive:** 'Don't be ridiculous! Of course you can't borrow my new camera—I paid a lot of money for it and I don't want it broken.'

- **Non-assertive:** 'Well, I don't like lending expensive things like this but if you promise to be careful with it I suppose it is all right.'

- **Assertive:** 'John, I'd rather not—the camera is too expensive to lend out.'

If assertiveness is that easy, then why aren't all people assertive? There are many reasons for people not acting assertively which, not surprisingly, vary from person to person. People may use non-assertive behaviour because:

They may suffer from low self-esteem and self-confidence. When people have low self-esteem or self-confidence, they will often devalue their own rights, believing that the needs of others are more important. Consequently they may make comments such as:

'But what will they think of me?'

'Am I being unreasonable?'

'I'll only get tongue-tied or embarrassed!'

'There are other people waiting to be served and I am holding them up.'

They may have a fear of conflict. Many people simply find the prospect of conflict too stressful. If their need to avoid conflict is high then they may give up their rights in order to avoid a stressful situation.

They lack the necessary assertiveness skills. Many people have not seen assertive behaviour used skilfully before. For example, if as a child they saw their parents deal with unacceptable behaviour with either non-assertive or aggressive behaviours, then this may become 'normal' behaviour for them too.

People may use aggressive behaviour because:

They may be confusing the person with the problem. For example, they might abuse an employee of a large chain store because a product purchased there was faulty. By the time the customer gets back to the place of purchase, they may end up venting their frustration on the first person who serves them instead of focusing their attention on the faulty product or service. Of course, in many cases the problem is not the fault of the person who sold us the product, yet if we are annoyed and inconvenienced they can become an easy scapegoat for our frustration.

They may be embarrassed. Sometimes people whose usual demeanour is meek will attempt to mask their lack of assertiveness skills by becoming aggressive. Unfortunately, they can then become so wound up due to their level of anxiety that they risk leaving without achieving their aim.

They may have a low tolerance for frustration. Some people are simply emotionally immature and have a correspondingly low tolerance for frustration. When things go wrong for them, it may bring on an emotional outburst. This could be caused by anything from a slow moving queue at the supermarket to the more serious issue of road rage when someone's driving behaviour annoys them. Often this behaviour stems from the poor coping behaviours that they saw modelled by their parents.

Assertive behaviour in relationships

As the date of retirement draws nearer, most people find themselves starting to imagine what their new lifestyle will be like. Discussion may centre around their plans for leisure activities, on 'the trip around Australia', or on drawing up budgets for maximising their lifestyles on a fixed income. However, very few people sit down before retirement and discuss the important subject of their need for individual space and autonomy.

Consequently, when the first day of retirement arrives, one partner may be expecting a lifestyle involving the emotional space to 'do their own thing' while the other partner may be envisaging a lifestyle where they do most things together. Clearly, these differing expectations need to be resolved if both people are to live mutually fulfilling lives; assertive behaviour is sometimes required to achieve this outcome.

Your relationship with friends and acquaintances are important partly because these people usually know you better than most others do; they may also be your link to important events and memories from years ago. Yet, ironically, close friends may feel that they can take liberties with you that others would not dream of taking. For example, an old friend who needs a golfing partner each Tuesday may expect you to fill that role even though they know that you would rather play less frequently. Consequently, you need to ensure that you assertively maintain your rights while still preserving old and irreplaceable friendships.

Participants in *Retire 200* identified five important relationship issues that they felt required the skilful use of assertive behaviour to manage.

Having your own space

'Husbands and wives should not live in each other's pockets—they need to have some interests apart, some time to themselves.'

Getting a partner to understand the importance to you of having physical and emotional space sometimes takes time and effort to achieve. For many people, this 'space' involves having a room in the house in which they can pursue hobbies or interests with minimal disruption. For others, it is an office or workshop.

'Create your own space—don't annoy your partner. Live independently from them to a degree.'

A number of people complained that when they expressed their need for some time alone, their partner would become offended and believed that their partner was tired of them! In particular, women found it annoying when their husband 'follows me around the house all day!' Another common issue arose where bored husbands volunteered to drive their wives to social engagements, thereby restricting their wives' freedom to act spontaneously and to choose how long they would stay at these events. These behaviours are sometimes referred to in sociological literature as 'the underfoot husband' phenomenon.

While the need to have their own space is usually resolved during the first twelve months of retirement, some people reported that working through the issue was not always easy. Misunderstandings and mistrust sometimes get in the way of intelligent, orderly discussion, and being able to assert one's rights skilfully as an individual is important at this time. A clear balance needs to be struck between giving up some rights to keep the peace and skilfully asserting the right to have appropriate periods of time to yourself.

Being free to 'do your own thing'

> 'I retired to keep my older retired husband company (at his insistence). I now do two hours voluntary work a week—I would like to do much more than this but my husband won't let me.'

I guess that many readers are now bristling with indignation: how could someone be so unreasonable! However, this story actually gets worse. Sadly, this woman felt so constricted by her husband's demands, and was so resentful about her plight that she claimed she was losing the will to live.

The powerful desire for freedom of activity relates to a strongly entrenched need as adults to be independent and to control their own lives. The lack of ability to skilfully assert her rights was not just annoying to this woman but had potentially become a matter of life and death.

Not being taken for granted

> 'Have a life of your own—don't be an on-call baby-sitter.'

While many people welcome the role of baby-sitter, others do not. Some people complained that their adult children made them feel guilty by citing what hard work life was these days. While manipulation of this type is obviously not acceptable, the fact remains that with child-minding costs escalating and couples working to pay off large mortgages, retired parents can become a convenient unpaid creche.

> *'I have four adult children, three sons and one daughter. One morning last year "good old Nana" found that she had six children to baby-sit that day—all were under the age of eight. By the time their parents collected them later that evening I was completely exhausted. At the age of sixty-two it was me that spat the dummy!'*

Where more than one adult child has children, some people described being forced to put their baby-sitting services on a roster simply because they could not cope with looking after all of their grandchildren at once. Relationships became strained when grandparents found themselves in the difficult situation of having to choose which of their grandchildren to baby-sit on a particular day. Insult was added to injury when, rather than being grateful for their retired parents' services, some adult children attempted to pressure them into taking the grandchildren more frequently.

Many of these problems can be avoided through the application of appropriate assertiveness on the part of the retired parents, and some empathy on the part of the adult children. Ways of being assertive in valued relationships, without creating World War III, are discussed later in this chapter.

Dealing with well-meaning friends and relatives who interfere

> *'Tell people who want you to do things to get lost. Do your own thing—retain your independence.'*

> *'Please yourself—don't act to meet others' expectations.'*

There is nothing more infuriating for an adult than to be told what is good for them or that 'what you should do is…'. It can be even harder to bite your tongue when well-meaning people offer you unsolicited advice when you are going through a period of significant change such as during adjustment to retirement. Effective assertiveness skills are necessary to ensure that you impress upon family and friends that retirement is your time to do what you like.

'Don't let others tell you what to do.'

One of the earliest lessons a first-year psychology student should receive is that *telling* people how to run their lives and how to solve their problems is a waste of time. The fact is that if personal problem-solving was that easy, someone would have written the *Solutions to Life's Problems* manual years ago and would now be sitting back counting their millions. Offering unsolicited advice, no matter how well intentioned, simply does not work because adults prefer to work through their own problems.

When serious attempts to resolve one's problems do not work, professional assistance from a psychologist or skilled counsellor can help. The psychologist/counsellor then acts as a facilitator who, rather than just providing an answer to the problem, provides the structure and objective feedback required to assist the person to arrive at a workable solution. Moreover, a secondary objective of professional counselling is to provide the client with a problem-solving model or process that they can then apply to future problems.

Ending relationships—'What! At my time of life!'

'Many people continue to drift along in dead or even violent relationships because they are fearful of leaving. "What would people think?" they ask.'

We are all familiar with stories of people staying in unsatisfactory marriages for the sake of the children. Even then, it is sometimes difficult to understand why a friend puts up with the ongoing hell they experience in their relationship. Clearly, it is a complicated area with few simple solutions.

It is tempting to imagine that by the time retirement comes along, most dysfunctional relationships would either have been sorted out or dissolved. Yet approximately 20 per cent of those people participating in *Retire 200* were not happy in their relationships (of course, this means that 80 per cent *were* happy which is probably a better way to view it!). The reasons given for persevering with poor relationships were many and varied:

◆ 'We both have our own interests so we hardly ever see each other.'

◆ 'We could not break up now! What would our children and friends think!'

◆ 'I have had a lover now for nearly twenty years—my husband does not know and I doubt whether he would care even if he found out. '

◆ 'We would both like to separate but we cannot afford to. '

◆ 'We did divorce some fifteen years ago but then remarried due to loneliness. Both of our marriages were mistakes!'

Deciding whether to remain in an unsatisfactory relationship or whether to leave is usually a complex process. Even where both parties are keen to separate, issues regarding finance and accommodation are important when income is typically less than it was when they were in the workforce.

For those of you reading this book and contemplating separation, it may be wise to seek professional advice from someone who is experienced in relationship counselling. The goal of professional relationship counsellors (once called marriage guidance counsellors) is not necessarily to preserve the relationship at all costs. Relationship counsellors will help you to identify and clarify the realities of your specific situation. The aim of the process is then for you both to arrive at a more objective assessment of whether your relationship is worth salvaging or not. Where it is, some change is usually required by both parties to repair the damage caused by previous dysfunctional behaviours.

Irrespective of whether you repair a flawed relationship or ultimately decide to end it, your ability to assert your rights will be important. If you stay together, assertiveness will be required to ensure that any agreed changes in behaviour actually take place and persist. If you separate, assertiveness will be required to attend to matters such as arranging new accommodation and ensuring that property is distributed equitably.

Improving your assertiveness skills

Assertive behaviour is simply the act of expressing your desires and needs openly and honestly. Consider the following example, which demonstrates the difference between assertive, non-assertive and aggressive behaviours.

◆ **Assertive behaviour:** 'I would like to use the car on Wednesday so that I can visit our grandchildren.'

◆ **Aggressive behaviour:** 'I'm going to use the car on Wednesday whether you like it or not. If you kick up a fuss about it, you can do your own cooking for the rest of the week.'

◆ **Non-assertive behaviour:** 'May I borrow the car on Wednesday—that is, if you don't think that you may want it yourself?'

When you are being assertive, it is not just a matter of using the right words. You also need to use assertive *non-verbal* behaviour (body language) to support your spoken language. The table contains a list of behaviours that assertive people use together with the non-assertive and aggressive equivalents.

Assertive behaviour	Non-assertive behaviour	Aggressive behaviour
Making eye contact to demonstrate that you mean what you say.	Looking away, or at your feet, when speaking.	Glaring and staring nastily.
Facing people squarely.	Turning your body away or moving back when speaking.	Moving quickly to the person, invading their personal space (getting too close), wagging your finger at them.
Matching facial expressions with the content of the message.	Using inappropriate expressions, for example, looking apologetic when requesting something that is your right.	Using inappropriate expressions, for example, frowning threateningly.
Speaking with appropriate volume.	Whispering or mumbling.	Yelling, screaming.

Assertive behaviour	Non-assertive behaviour	Aggressive behaviour
Using active-case 'I' statements, for example, 'I would like you to help me tidy up the house before our friends arrive.'	Using passive-case statements, for example, 'It would be nice if the house could be tidied up before our friends arrive.'	Getting personal, for example, 'Tidy up the house. I am sick and tired of your sloppy ways.'

Knowing what assertiveness comprises is one thing; actually being assertive is another! People who have difficulty with this usually know what they would like to say but are unable to actually say it.

So how do you develop the skills you need to express your feelings, and to get your rights in relationships? One solution frequently used by psychologists is to teach their clients the three step process of behavioural rehearsal.

Step 1. Think of an issue that is bothering you because you have not assertively addressed it with the person involved. If you cannot think of an issue, make one up for the purpose of the exercise, for example,

> *'Since we have retired, my husband and I have had Sue and Mike around for dinner three times in a row, yet they keep on coming around without any apparent intention of returning our hospitality. I find that I am getting resentful, and it is starting to affect how I feel about Sue. If I don't raise the issue with her soon, this resentment will get worse.'*

Step 2. Plan how you will confront Sue in a socially acceptable yet assertive manner, for example,

> *'Sue, John and I were saying the other day that we have not been around to your place for dinner for ages. Why don't we get together soon—I have lots to tell you.'*

You may be wondering why we are not saying something like,

> *'Sue, John and I were saying the other night that we can't understand why it is that despite us having you around for dinner three times in a row, you have never returned the invitation!'*

There are two reasons for using the first approach with Sue:

◆ Your friends Sue and Mike may genuinely believe that accepting three consecutive dinners at your place does not constitute unreasonable behaviour and may be planning to invite you to their home for the next dinner.

◆ As they are friends, the goal of the exercise is to be diplomatically assertive while retaining the friendship.

Some psychologists refer to this diplomacy as using the 'minimal effective response' technique, that is, achieving your desired outcome without unwanted side effects.

Using the minimal effective response technique is also a good idea when dealing with awkward issues with a neighbour. For example, saying something like the following is assertive but probably inappropriate:

'I have consulted the by-laws officer and he tells me that under Section 234 (i) (a), I have the right to have your dog destroyed if it continues to bark at night. Please rectify the situation immediately.'

Step 3. Having selected an issue with which to rehearse your assertive behaviours, design or script your statement using the above examples to get some ideas on how to structure your approach.

Practise your delivery aloud in front of a mirror. Alternatively, you can ask your partner or a friend to role play with you, or you could go through this exercise with a psychologist if you are seeing one. By rehearsing aloud or with a 'coach' present you give yourself the opportunity to hear what your communication would sound like. You can then adjust your choice of words, timing or manner of speech according to what you hear yourself saying, or according to the advice of your coach. While you are rehearsing, remember to also attend to your assertive non-verbal behaviours (body language).

Just as rehearsals for a play or a concert do not always result in perfect performances, you may find that some people respond to you with rudeness or by ignoring your request. There is no need for you to feel that you have failed. You have already done well simply by demonstrating your desire to assert your rights, especially if this has been a problem for you in the past.

Remember, there are *two* goals to assertive behaviour:

◆ to assert your desire for your rights to be respected (for your self-esteem), and

◆ to actually achieve your rights (as a human being).

Even where people choose not to act on your requests, or where they meet your approach with rudeness, you will still have achieved the goal of establishing and requesting your rights. This in itself is important for your continued self-esteem and shows that you are someone who is prepared to stand up for themselves.

Assertiveness strategies

Although it is very important to obtain your rights, not all of the people you approach will welcome your request—particularly where they have a strong emotional or financial interest in preserving the status quo. Where you encounter such resistance, you can try the following strategies.

Use distraction to prevent someone from discussing your personal affairs

If someone is moving the topic of the conversation to a personal matter that you do not wish to discuss, try using distraction:

'You mentioned before that since you have retired you have set up a workshop under your house. What sort of things do you make there?'

OR

'I hear you have been overseas recently. How did you enjoy the trip?'

Change the subject when you are not comfortable with the topic

A friend who is visiting you may start discussing details of a terminal illness that a friend is suffering from. As you feel that continued discussion of the topic will be upsetting, your assertive response could be:

'Anne, that subject is a little upsetting. I would rather talk about something else if you don't mind.'

OR

'Anne, do you mind if we discuss something else?'

Wind up an inappropriate or boring conversation

You can end an inappropriate conversation by using non-verbal (body language) cues to indicate that you are now no longer interested in talking. Turning away slightly and/or looking off into the distance often helps get the message across. If this does not work then try saying something like:

'I should go and catch up with Fred now—there are a couple of things we need to discuss.'

OR

'Time is marching on—I'd better go and get the shopping done.'

Deal with a nagger using the 'fog' technique

The fog technique is effective when dealing with someone who nags you, or who tries to force their views on you. The fog technique involves communicating to them that they *may* be right, or that they *could* be right. You cloud or 'fog' the issue by not actually telling them they *are* right. An example of this would be:

Jack:	'Lyn tells me you are getting a painter in to go over the house. You know, now that you are retired you should do this yourself—you will save a fortune!'
Brian:	'Yes, it would save money but quite frankly I hate painting and I can afford to pay for it.'
Jack:	'Yes, but now that you have the time you would probably find that you would enjoy the challenge.'
Brian:	'You may be right.' (fog)
Jack:	'Of course I am right! You could go on a trip with the money you save.'
Brian:	'Hmm! Well, you could be right.' (fog)

In most cases, using the fog technique will eventually cause the nagger to run out of steam. However, if they persist in annoying you, try the following:

Jack:	'What's all this "you may be right" stuff—why don't you just admit that I am right!'
Brian:	'I don't agree with you. Let's change the subject.'

Again, the two goals here are to assert your right not to agree, and to maintain the self-esteem and friendship of your partner or friend.

Achieve your rights in business dealings

While modern consumer laws and competitive business practices have in many instances softened the old 'let the buyer beware' attitudes of years ago, poor customer service remains a problem. Some business people will resist meeting their obligations by trying to fob you off when you request what is rightfully yours. Consequently, you can find that rectifying unsatisfactory service takes resolve and determination to achieve.

The key is to say to yourself, 'I am not asking for anything unreasonable here—it is my right to get the goods and services that I pay for.' Once you have this firmly fixed in your mind, it becomes much easier to approach the shop assistant or business person and to simply and calmly request a satisfactory outcome.

Customer:	'I'd like to return this shirt — the stitching around the collar is faulty.'
Retailer:	'Let's see! Oh dear, I can hardly see it! Nobody will notice that, it's just a very small imperfection.'
Customer:	'Yes it is small but it is an imperfection and I would like to exchange it, please.'
Retailer:	'Well, I'm afraid that was the last one. We will be getting another delivery in about eight weeks—give me your phone number and I'll call you then.'
Customer:	'I bought the shirt to wear now. If you can't

	replace it now I would like my money back.'
Retailer:	'Well, we don't usually refund money on returned articles.'
Customer (ignoring this ploy):	'Fine—here is my credit card for the refund.'

The customer remains polite and reasonable while assertively requesting their rights. There is no need to become heated, angry or upset. Just as important here is the use of non-verbal behaviour (body language). It is the combination of direct and honest verbal with non-verbal assertive behaviour that provides the full power of assertive behaviour.

Diffuse a person's anger

Unfortunately, some relationships involve abuse. If you believe you are in danger, or have been attacked by the person before, you need to seek help from an appropriate source. Depending on the type or severity of the problem, this assistance could range from one or both parties attending counselling to police action.

If you are not sure who to turn to, there are a number of agencies that can provide assistance that is usually free of charge. For example, telephone-based crisis referral agencies will point you in the right direction.

In the meantime, diffusing anger is important if unpleasantness is to be avoided. The following example shows how an assertive person may diffuse anger:

George:	'You idiot—why can't you learn to control your spending? We are retired now, you know!'
Mary:	'You are obviously very angry. Let's sit down and talk about it.'
George :	'Talking is not going to help. You've run up a large bill on our credit card. When will you stop wasting our money?'
Mary:	'I'd like to discuss this with you but it is really difficult when you keep yelling at me.'

George:	'I want this spending to cease right now—we can't afford to get into debt. We'll lose the house, everything!'
Mary:	'Then let's sit down and talk about it.'
George:	'Okay, okay—so why did you run up the debt on our credit card last week?'

By remaining calm and demonstrating that she wanted to resolve the issue, Mary assertively brought George's anger down to a manageable level from which she could begin an orderly discussion.

Warning: If you are in any physical danger, or if you are in a situation where alcohol or drugs are playing a role in the anger, it is wiser not to push for your rights until the situation is safe. Withdrawal from the area or the person is usually the best advice.

Use the 'broken record' technique when you are being pressured to agree to something against your will

Have you ever experienced the pressure of a well-meaning but insistent friend or relative who wants you to do something, or to go somewhere, that does not interest you? Sometimes it can be tempting to just give in and go along with them, however, there are times when you simply will not want to take part in somebody else's plans.

The following example shows how to use the broken record technique to assert your right not to agree:

Paul:	'Damien, I've just bought a new boat. I'm taking you out fishing tomorrow afternoon.'
Damien:	'Thanks for the offer, Paul, but I don't feel all that comfortable in boats.'
Paul:	'Oh, you don't have to worry—it's a safe boat and I am an experienced sailor.'
Damien:	'Paul, I have no doubts about your expertise nor about the safety of your boat—I just don't enjoy being in them.'

Paul:	'That's because you have probably been out in smaller boats with inexperienced people. I promise you that everything will be okay.'
Damien	(using the broken record technique): 'As I say, I have no doubts about your expertise nor the safety of your boat—I just don't enjoy being in them. I'll catch up with you over the weekend for a beer.'

In the above example, Damien would keep applying the broken record technique until Paul finally got the message. By 'softening' the process with the suggestion of catching up later for a beer, Damien achieves the joint goals of asserting his rights, and maintaining Paul's self-esteem and friendship.

The broken record technique can also be used where you wish to get rid of high-pressure salespeople who are invading your privacy or wasting your time. Of course, here you could just (aggressively) hang up the telephone or shut the door in their face, but most people do not feel comfortable doing this. The broken record technique allows you to assertively manage the situation:

Telephone salesperson:	'... and once you have used our lawn fertiliser your grass will always be greener.'
Customer:	'I'm not interested, thank you.'
Telephone salesperson:	'If you buy our product I'll throw in an introductory fifteen per cent discount. You will never go back to any other product.'
Customer:	'No thanks, I am not interested.'
Telephone salesperson:	'Your next door neighbour uses our products and he swears by them.'
Customer (using the broken record technique):	'No thanks, I am not interested.'

In these circumstances there are no relationship issues to preserve or nurture so you can just keep repeating 'No thanks, I am not interested' until the message sinks in. If the salesperson does not get the message after your repeated responses, you can say, 'No thanks—I am going to hang up now,' then just hang up.

CHECKLIST

❑ I understand the differences between aggressive behaviour, non-assertive behaviour and assertive behaviour.

❑ I will rehearse assertive behaviour to improve my levels of assertiveness.

❑ I am familiar with the seven assertiveness techniques described in this chapter.

Chapter 4

Resolving conflict and negotiating good deals

The aims of this chapter are to:

◆ understand why conflict resolution and negotiation skills are important in retirement;

◆ identify what goes wrong when conflict resolution and negotiation fails; and

◆ provide guidelines for use during conflict or negotiation.

The importance of conflict resolution and negotiation skills

Why would anyone need to be concerned about conflict management or negotiation in retirement? Surely retirement is a time for relaxing, having fun and doing your own thing! On the other hand, could it be that even in retirement, Malcolm Fraser's words 'Life was not meant to be easy' still apply? Effective conflict resolution and negotiation skills are helpful in three areas of life.

Relations with your partner/spouse

There have been numerous studies pointing to an increased rate of marital separation in the years immediately following retirement, probably because partners can find that they have each other's undivided attention for the first time in many years. Conflict resolution skills can help partners work through any relationship problems that surface due to the

The subject of ongoing arguments between partners was raised frequently by those in the research program. The most common causes of disputes, where both partners were retired, concerned:

◆ the use of leisure time;

◆ finances—how much to spend and what to spend it on;

◆ the need of one partner to have time and space to themselves;

◆ whether to move from the family home or not; and

◆ accepting responsibility for maintenance, cleaning and other essential duties around the home.

As the various styles of decision-making are looked at it is interesting to note that the style you use when trying to win arguments is often drawn from those you saw your parents use when they were arguing. Consequently, your expectation of what is effective and what is not may be based on the style of the parent you saw winning most of the arguments. For example, was the 'winner' quiet, measured and reasonable, did they yell, cry, and scream, did they use clever linguistic ability and logic to win arguments or did the loudest parent always seem to win the argument?

Ineffective conflict resolution

There are four common but ineffective styles that people may adopt when attempting to resolve conflict:

Style 1: Aggressors

Aggressors are typified by these behaviours:

◆ Winning is the only acceptable outcome—there are few rules and strategies may include physical or psychological violence.

◆ Screaming, yelling and threatening.

◆ Cold logic is applied even if this clearly ignores the emotional needs of the other person.

◆ It is not important if the vanquished is happy about the outcome or not.

special stresses affecting them as they adjust to their new lifestyle. teething problems are addressed early they are less likely to develop int major difficulties.

Friends and neighbours

The lifestyles of friends and neighbours, which were barely noticed when you were at work during the day, may now escalate into a range of annoying, intrusive behaviours. These annoyances will require careful resolution if neighbourly relationships are to remain intact and everyone is to stay calm.

Business dealings

For most people, retirement represents a time when financial status shifts from the wealth accumulation phase to the wealth management phase. Consequently, negotiation skills are important when it comes to buying a new home, purchasing a car or any of the other necessities of life.

Roles, responsibilities and territorial disputes

'. . . and,' she said with a note of concern in her voice, 'After he retires next Friday, he is going to be here... all the time!'

Retirement can trigger special pressures where marriage relationships have comprised older-style 'traditional' husband and wife roles where the husband is the principal breadwinner. In such relationships, wives of recently retired men frequently complain that they find their former roles and responsibilities are now devalued by a well-meaning but bored and interfering husband. For example, the weekly shopping has been known to become a battleground with arguments in the supermarket as the newly retired partner removes items from the trolley in exchange for a 'cheaper' brand.

Arguments

'Since my husband retired it seems that we have done nothing but argue and bicker, sometimes over the silliest things. It drives us both nuts but we keep going round and round in circles without resolving anything.'

When arguments are won in this way, the aggressive winner may feel good for a short time, however, such victories are not really 'won' in the long term. Eventually the loser is likely to start applying 'passive' aggression such as moping about or showing their resentment and anger in other ways. Consequently, if the vanquished is unhappy in the relationship, then life will soon become miserable for the aggressor too. In other words, the aggressor might win the battle using this method but they will not win the war!

Style 2: Peacemakers

Peacemakers are typified by these behaviours:

- ◆ They fear situations where discussions appear to be about to escalate into an argument.
- ◆ They have a high need to keep interactions polite and unheated.
- ◆ They give in to others' demands to calm things down and maintain the peace.

Peacemakers feel better in the short term because the perceived unpleasantness has dissipated. However, it will eventually occur to them that they have sacrificed what is rightfully theirs and they will come to resent the fact that their partner does not really have their interests at heart. Like those who lose to the 'Aggressors,' they will often resort to passive aggression by regularly harping about their good-natured preparedness to back down. Their aim is to make the winner feel guilty and nobody really wins in the long term.

Style 3: Avoiders

Avoiders are typified by these behaviours:

- ◆ They avoid conflict at all costs.
- ◆ They will change the subject to avoid confrontation.
- ◆ They try to distract the other person by introducing a 'safer' topic to try and get them off contentious subjects.
- ◆ They will sometimes physically leave the room to avoid conflict.

Avoiders find that their anxiety diminishes in the short term. However, any ongoing problems between the avoider and the other person remain unresolved. Consequently, the problem continues to bubble under the surface and will re-emerge to disrupt the relationship at some other time.

For those living around avoiders, the situation can be equally frustrating. Issues that are annoying them, and which they would prefer to discuss or bring to a head, continue to impact on the relationship. Again, there are no winners when this style of problem solving is used.

Style 4: Givers and takers

The major behaviour pattern of givers and takers is that they compromise on the understanding that the other party compromises too. To a casual observer, the process used by givers and takers appears to be fair and reasonable. However, in reality nobody wins and nobody loses. Everyone acts and feels terribly civilised, but both parties go away frustrated by their attempts to resolve the problem. Consequently, the problem blows up again the next time the issue arises.

Developing conflict resolution and negotiation skills

Conflict resolution and negotiation skills share a number of steps and processes in common; both sets of skills involve applying a range of interpersonal processes so that mutually agreeable outcomes result. The key difference between the two, however, is that in the case of negotiation skills the event is usually yet to occur, for example, selling a house or negotiating the best price for a car. In conflict resolution, the event or the decision has usually already occurred with negative consequences for one or both parties, for example, a dispute between neighbours over the disturbance caused by a barking dog.

Another significant difference between the two processes can relate to the level of the interpersonal relationships involved. In negotiation, the relationship is:

◆ usually either nonexistent (for example, purchasing a house from a stranger), or

◆ at least functional (for example, negotiating with members of the extended family regarding who is going to use a shared holiday house at Easter).

Conflict resolution involves arriving at agreement on a subject that has become highly emotionally charged and where the relationship of the parties involved is either ailing or has broken down altogether.

Improving conflict resolution skills

It can be helpful to view conflict as a natural outcome of the differing views and opinions that people hold. In most cases, society's diverse opinions and attitudes enrich our environment by promoting variety. For example, if you sent twelve people into a shop and instructed them to buy a 'tasteful' necktie, the range of ties purchased would be diverse. Unfortunately, the very same diversity that promotes cultural and artistic richness also extends to opinions regarding the correct height of neighbours' fences, the acceptable frequency of a dog's bark and the levels of noise from late-night parties next door.

In Australia, there is now a growth industry dedicated to providing professional services in the area of conflict resolution. Since the early 1990s, a number of municipalities have offered conflict resolution services to assist in the settlement of disputes among neighbours. At a commercial level, there are also legal firms offering similar dispute resolution services for issues arising between businesses and their clients.

Of course, there is little doubt that when it comes to managing conflict, prevention is better than cure. However, as disagreements are inevitable where people with differing interests and values interact, it is important that we are all able to manage conflict. If we can also view it as an opportunity for growth then so much the better!

The win-win concept

Modern conflict resolution involves applying what has become known as the win-win concept. This process has proven to be so successful that the term 'win-win' has now entered everyday language and is used to describe practically any interaction between people where nobody is disadvantaged.

Win-win works on the premise that if people involved in a dispute discuss their needs collectively and work together to find a solution that meets their individual interests, it is possible to reach a conclusion where everyone's needs are met. In other words, nobody loses—hence win-win.

An example of win-win at a very basic level could involve a shift-worker who needs to sleep during the day when the retiree next door chooses to play loud music on his CD player. One person needs to sleep; one person is exercising their right to play music during the day. In the example, resolution of this conflict is attempted unsuccessfully by using the compromise model, and then successfully by using the win-win model.

Compromise model

Retiree (asked to compromise by turning down the volume):	'But if I turn down my amplifier I can't hear the rhythm section clearly; and anyway rock is meant to be loud—it's not background music!'
Shift-worker (asked to sleep in a room on the other side of the house during the day):	'My wife and children use the other rooms and my sleeping on that side of the house would inconvenience them—working night shift is bad enough as it is!'

Win-win model

Retiree:	'When I am playing CDs I will close the two windows on your side of my house as well as the connecting door from the loungeroom to the room nearest your side of the house.'
Shift-worker:	'... and I'll shut my bedroom window.'

Meeting interests rather than positions

When people are in conflict they invariably come up with their own 'position' quite early in the process. One neighbour might say,

'I must have a high fence for privacy.'

The other neighbour might say,

'I can't tolerate high fences—they make me feel like I'm in a prison.'

Once these opinions are aired they can be difficult to back away from gracefully. Conflict resolution experts refer to such rigidity of thinking as 'arguing from a position'. On the other hand, when the win-win process is applied the parties in the dispute are encouraged to identify their real needs. In win-win parlance, these needs are called 'interests'.

Interests include our concerns, wants and needs and are usually the real reason for the dispute in the first place. For example, when one neighbour takes the position 'I must have a high fence', their real interest might be 'I want privacy.' Likewise when the other neighbour takes the position, 'I could not bear a high fence', their real interest may be, 'I want natural light in my kitchen and hobbies room.' Therefore, when we negotiate with the aim of meeting everyone's interests we open up a range of possible options from which we can select one that works for all parties.

Following are some compelling reasons for concentrating on interests rather than on positions.

The cycle of bickering. When people argue regularly, particularly within a close relationship, they sometimes fall into the habit of never genuinely attempting to resolve the dispute. It may be that the argument started out over who should take out the rubbish or who should vacuum the house. Unfortunately, over time, the argument may deteriorate into a contest to see who gives in first! On the other hand, if the discussion centres on each other's interests and both people start looking for a win-win, then the pressure to keep fighting dissipates.

If the situation concerns rubbish removal or vacuuming then the real issue or interest may be about the equitable division of labour around the house now that both partners have retired from the workforce. Arguing from positions may see the husband saying,

'But my wife has always done the vacuuming—why should I start doing it now?'

His wife may be saying,

'But that was when you were working full-time and I was only working two days a week. It's your turn now!'

If the partners were to focus on interests, in this case, the equitable division of labour, then they could generate a list of the important jobs that need doing around the house and agree to split them up fairly. It may then turn out that the husband takes over the vacuuming while his wife washes the car, or that she continues to vacuum while he takes on other responsibilities such as hanging out the washing.

Permanency. Another dilemma common in relationship disputes occurs where the same old argument repeatedly resurfaces. This situation invariably occurs where people are arguing from positions and the only way to end the argument is for one person to lose, or for both to compromise. The result is that no one is truly satisfied and the real problem-solving process ends up being perpetually postponed.

Say for example that one partner likes to watch the football on television on Saturday afternoons yet finds that his wife hates the raucous background noise of the sporting commentators. If a compromise solution was used, such as turning the volume down low, neither party would really be satisfied; the football fan would be straining to hear the match details and may feel that the atmosphere of the game was being lost, while his wife would still be annoyed by being able to hear the irritating commentary, albeit at a lower volume.

By discussing their respective interests, a mutually satisfying solution could be found. For example, the husband could buy a set of high-quality lightweight stereo headphones with which to listen to the match. The needs and interests of both parties would then be met.

Versatility. Another reason for focusing on interests is the sheer range of potential options that become available when solutions are examined collaboratively. When people begin to work as a team, they enhance their ability to think creatively and to generate options for meeting everyone's interests. Clearly, the more potential options that become available, the greater the likelihood of finding a solution that is aligned to the interests of all parties.

Suggested guidelines for conflict resolution

In my own dealings with clients I have found the following points to be helpful. They are an amalgam of the procedures used by modern practitioners of conflict resolution.

Setting the right environment for discussion

Before arranging the meeting with the others involved in the dispute, give some thought to how and where you will hold the meeting. The venue needs to be on neutral territory so that no one feels at an advantage or disadvantage. A very natural reaction when we are under stress is to want to physically escape from the situation. This reaction is known as 'flight or fight' and is powerfully installed in the primitive limbic system of the brain. It is therefore not wise to hold the meeting in a small stuffy room where people may feel hemmed in during stressful moments.

Creating the right physical environment is only one part of the equation; it is also important that the right psychological and social environment is created. Therefore, while you may not be feeling terribly charitable towards the people involved in the dispute, try to go out of your way to put them at ease and to make them feel safe. Encourage them to feel that the process will be worth their while. Before getting into the main discussion, tell them that you are confident that by working together, you and they will come up with some ideas that will be mutually acceptable.

Clarify everyone's perceptions of what the conflict is really about

Take all the time necessary to establish what the core issues of conflict are. Remember not to confuse the *person* with the *problem*. For example, it is not your *neighbour* who is causing you stress, but the fact that a high fence may *block out the natural light* to your kitchen.

It is also a good idea to discuss who is going to have their say first. Have everyone agree that once someone is having their turn to talk, they should be allowed to speak uninterrupted. This process allows everyone to get their issues out into the open and to feel that they have been heard. It can also break new ground by allowing people to hear each other's perceptions of the problem, possibly for the first time!

When deciding who is to start the discussion, offer the other person the opportunity to speak first. In some instances, particularly where trust between the parties is very low, the other person may wish you to go first for fear that you may capitalise on their disclosure. If you sense this is their concern, then by all means go first.

Use language carefully

Be careful about how you structure your language so that you do not inadvertently sound as if you are in 'blaming' mode. For example, instead of saying 'You are making my life miserable', say 'It will be difficult for me if I have to work in artificial light in my kitchen.'

Ask questions to ensure that you are clear about how the other person perceives the problem. Then, listen carefully to what everyone says and provide feedback to them that demonstrates you are hearing and understanding the content of their message (see Chapter 2 for more information about attending skills). As you listen, try to empathise with their position; reassess whether YOU are being completely honest and reasonable. Where you find that you have entered the discussion with an erroneous perception of the situation, be honest and disclose this to them.

Encourage collaborative effort

Try to encourage a team approach to solving the dispute; the conflict will not be resolved until all parties genuinely and completely support proposed solutions. It can be very easy at this time for one or more people in the dispute to dominate by using their strength of personality against a less powerful person. If the discussions then conclude in apparent agreement which is really due to dominance at the discussion table, the 'agreement' will be short-lived and will collapse once all parties are back on their own territories. Lasting decisions only occur where everyone's interests are considered and where a process of collaborating to generate options for moving forward is genuinely agreed.

Look forward instead of dwelling on the past

Like most of the components of conflict resolution, looking forward demands a certain degree of generosity from all parties. Dwelling on past events, skirmishes or insults will not help move the process towards an effective outcome. Therefore, agree together to try to focus on the problem as it is now. Resist the temptation to drag up the details of old disagreements, particularly where they focus on some of the less attractive aspects of human nature.

A further goal in effective conflict resolution should be to not only address the issues, but to try to restore the relationships between those who may now not be on comfortable speaking terms. Once the relationship has been re-established, any further issues that arise can be more easily resolved without escalating into yet another dispute.

Develop a range of possible options

As options are being generated, keep an open mind and try not to be too quick to discount the ideas of others. Ask for the other party's contributions first and acknowledge the positive aspects of their suggestions. Suggest using a brain-storming approach, that is, have a session where ideas and options are generated to meet the interests of everyone, but where critical discussion or rejection of ideas is postponed until the list is complete.

When going through the list of options generated, encourage each other to look for common threads and then work together on the suggestions that seem most likely to satisfy everyone's needs.

Generate a list of agreed actions

This is one of the most important stages in the conflict resolution process, where everyone starts to agree on some small steps that they can move forward with before resolving the main issue. For example, if you and your partner are dealing with a wide range of issues that are affecting your happiness, then the 'one small step at a time' strategy is a wise idea. Trying to radically change the complex dynamics of a relationship overnight is unlikely to work and will just serve to diminish everyone's belief that change is possible.

Write an agreement that summarises the benefits

Once there is agreement from all parties concerning the way forward, it is important to draw up a written list of the agreed actions or decisions. Next to this list, write a brief description of the benefits to each person concerned in the dispute. (Where actions such as building a fence are involved, it is important to ensure that completion dates are built into the agreement so that the solution is not avoided by one party.) The following is an example of an action statement.

Action statement
1.   We have agreed to build a wooden fence 175 cm high.
2.   We will obtain at least three quotes from reputable fencing contractors.
3.   We will meet by 15 March to decide which contractor will get the work.
4.   The construction of the fence is to be commenced by 30 April.

Benefits
For Julie: Natural light will continue to reach the kitchen and hobbies room.
For Peter: A 175 cm fence will provide privacy and will stop my young children from gaining access to the busy road through Julie's property.

Julie Street .... Peter Jones................................

Once the agreement is drawn up and signed, everyone should be given a copy to retain. If memories about what was agreed blur later, the action statement provides the evidence required.

Dealing with emotions during conflict resolution

The methods for resolving conflict, described above, have long been applied successfully by professionals. However, for those who have never engaged in conflict resolution before, the prospect can feel quite threatening. This is particularly true where the conflict has been drawn out over time, and where those involved have allowed the situation to deteriorate to personal accusations and insults. Under these circumstances, it is understandable when people become apprehensive about their ability to deal with emotions such as anger and resentment — either their own, or that of others.

The following sections look at ways in which you can handle your own emotions and those of others during the dispute resolution process.

Focus on the problem

'Leaving your ego at the door' is highly recommended when you are entering into dispute resolution. If you allow your ego and feelings to take over you will soon find that they interfere with the real goal of the exercise, which is to focus on solving the problem.

The following ego-based emotional reactions are among those that most often block effective conflict resolution.

- **Reacting defensively:** for example, interpreting comments expressed about the problem as a personal attack.

- **Point scoring:** for example, throwing in cheap shots of a personal nature but which have little to do with solving the actual problem.

- **Accusing:** for example, implying that the problem is mainly the fault of the other person.

- **Going on the attack:** for example, attempting to undermine the confidence of others by a personal attack, 'If you had not (done such and such) everything would be okay.'

Handling outbursts of anger from the other party

When people are angry or hurt they may resort to a personal verbal attack. It is very easy, especially during the heat of the moment, to take these comments personally and to respond in kind. However, self-indulgent responses of this type usually signal the end to any meaningful discussion, at least until everyone has had time to calm down again. Unfortunately, in the meantime, more ruminating and brooding will usually have occurred and gaining a successful resolution to the problem becomes even more difficult to achieve.

If you find that the other party is becoming angry, there are a number of steps that you can take to help diffuse their anger. Understand, however, that applying these steps takes a hefty degree of emotional maturity, generosity and self-discipline on your part:

Let them get the matter off their chest. In counselling circles this process is known as 'venting'. It allows the other person to release some of the built-up anger and resentment they have been bottling up. It is important during this time to resist the natural urge to interrupt; just listen to them quietly and try to convey the impression that you are not judging them. To convey this non-judgmental impression you need to be aware of your non-verbal language, such as not raising your eyebrows at their comments, not smirking and not appearing smug.

Try not to react defensively. Whether it is intended or not, people will sometimes use language that can easily be taken personally as you listen to them describe the problem. For example, instead of saying, 'I get upset when I think about the natural light I will lose if a high fence goes up' they may say, 'The thought of you building your stupid fence is causing me a lot of stress.' It is very easy to find yourself bristling when you are on the receiving end of this type of language. Try to put their remarks in the context of the real concerns they are trying to convey, and the emotions they are experiencing.

Managing your own emotions

There are a number of steps that you can take to manage your own emotions during the resolution process:

Preparation. Make a list of your interests so that they are clear and accessible when you are under pressure. Even the most eloquent speaker can become tongue-tied during the heat of the moment; having a list in front of you will help you to remain focused on the important points.

List the points you believe the other person will raise. The thinking behind this idea is that it helps you to see the situation as they may be seeing it. You may then find it easier to see the dispute in terms of interests rather than perpetuating the blaming stance that can result from only looking at the issues from your own position.

Rehearse relaxation techniques. Here you can apply an abbreviated version of the diaphragmatic breathing exercises described in Chapter 10. The method of relaxation described here differs slightly from the process described in that chapter in that it can be used if you find yourself getting heated *during* the resolution process.

(a) Slowly take a deep breath and hold it in for a couple of seconds.
(b) Tell yourself to relax and then slowly breathe out again.
(c) Relax your muscles as you breathe. Say to yourself, 'I am relaxing and staying calm.'
(d) Refocus your mind and energy on the process of resolving the conflict.

Sometimes, despite your best intentions, you may find yourself losing control of your emotions. It may be that you are mulling over something someone has said, and which you have interpreted as an insult. However, as we discussed earlier, it is not helpful to react at the same level. Remaining cool in the face of provocative behaviour will enhance your credibility in the eyes of all of those present.

There are three steps you can take to convey the impression that you are in control, even if inwardly you feel like exploding. These methods are very powerful and are used extensively by negotiation and conflict resolution specialists:

◆ Focus on interests. Take a deep breath and continue to focus on interests rather than on getting even with the other person.

◆ Interpret insults as unintentional. Give the other person the benefit of the doubt even if you are privately convinced that their comments were designed to hurt or annoy you. You may have misunderstood them, but in any case putting a generous interpretation on their words will help you achieve the real goal of solving the problem.

◆ Act as if you are relaxed. Simply acting as if you are relaxed helps you return to a more stable emotional level. On the other hand, succumbing to your feelings is likely to result in you winding yourself up even further. By staying calm in the face of the other person, you reduce the likelihood of them becoming angry too.

The following steps will help you to act, and then become, calm:

◆ Maintain your normal volume when speaking.

◆ Try to keep your voice even so that any hurt or exasperation does not show.

◆ Remember to maintain appropriate eye contact—if you suddenly start redirecting your gaze elsewhere or looking down while you speak, you will alert the other person to your discomfort.

◆ Do not fidget or wave your hands around.

Improving negotiation skills

When you are negotiating with family or friends ('Let's go to a movie' versus 'Let's go out for dinner'), you can also apply the win-win techniques that were discussed in the above section on conflict resolution.

There will be situations, however, where the person or organisation you are dealing with is not interested in your goodwill or in behaving ethically. They are simply focused on getting your money and as much of it as possible!

The following section examines some ways in which you can beat hard-headed, rough, tough negotiators at their own game. For the purposes of this discussion the example of buying a car is used because nearly everyone will need to buy a car at some time during their retirement and because the sales strategies used in the car sales industry are about as tough as they get.

These comments are bound to draw responses from car salespeople such as, 'But we are not like that any more' or 'We are customer-focused these days!' To be a little generous, let us acknowledge that there are good, reputable car salespeople out there. In fact, in the case of large dealerships, a large component of their future cash stream can come from providing the ongoing service and maintenance of your car, so there is a strong vested interest in keeping you on side as a potential service customer. However, visit a second-hand car lot and you are still likely to find yourself in a tough environment where after-sales service ranges from low on their corporate priorities to nonexistent.

Know your adversary

When you are negotiating with tough business people, there is much you can do to establish the balance of power in your favour. The old saying 'Knowledge is power' is particularly apt in these circumstances. Therefore, DO YOUR HOMEWORK! For example, when the car industry was researched for this section of the book, three car salespeople were consulted. They revealed the following facts about the ways in which car salespeople may operate:

1. The remuneration of car salespeople is usually by sales commission. If they don't sell they don't get paid, so they are under great pressure to make sales. Think back to when you were working in the full-time workforce. How would you have reacted if the boss suddenly told you that your next pay cheque would only be delivered if you brought in new customers to the organisation?

2. In the car sales business only the tough survive—even other car sales-

people want their colleagues to fail so that more of the potential customers who walk into the car yard are *theirs*!

3. Car salespeople attend seminars, listen to audio tapes, watch video tapes and talk with other salespeople on the topic of how to get the sale. 'Getting the sale' means getting your signature on a contract and getting the money. However, it is not likely that many of them attend seminars on 'How to provide superb customer service and ensure customer satisfaction.'

4. In some car sales businesses, the salesperson who sells the least number of cars for the month or quarter 'leaves' and a new salesperson takes their place.

5. Car salespeople are highly competitive and, apart from making money, are often motivated by winning the car yard's salesperson of the month or other recognition-based sales competition. The winner of these competitions is not the salesperson that customers nominate for providing the best service, but the one who sells the most cars.

6. Customers who are considerate, polite and who do not try to drive a hard bargain are often derisively referred to as 'wood-ducks' due to their lack of aggression or strategies to 'avoid capture'.

7. Car salespeople and the concept of after-sales service are frequently at opposite ends of the continuum. Customers who return to speak to the salesperson because they are unhappy with the car they have purchased may be referred to as 'ghosts' because they come back to haunt the salesperson with problems.

What they know about you

By doing some basic research, you can gain information that gives you inside knowledge which is important as you negotiate. For example, if you had thought that the car salesperson received a salary, you may have approached them differently than you would if you understood the financial pressure they are under to make sales. It is also important to know how they operate because, within a few minutes of you walking into a car yard, they know much about you and your individual buying behaviours. For example:

- They already know you would love to buy a new car no matter how blasé you try to look! You would not be there if you were not at least interested in the idea of a new car.

- They are trained to look for buying signals. For example, if you touch the car while you are discussing it, it could be interpreted as meaning that you are starting to regard the car as your own property. Other signals you give away can be verbal: 'Can you get these with cruise control?' Why would you ask that if you were not interested in the car?

- They carefully watch your non-verbal (body) language. For example, a furtive smile of approval to your partner as the salesperson brings the price down closer to your budget.

- Car salespeople who have been in the industry for a while pick up signals from you that even *they* would have difficulty in explaining! It seems that when a customer is ready to buy, they unwittingly display an array of verbal and non-verbal buying signals that give the game away. These all indicate to the salesperson that it is time to move in and make the sale.

Know the seller's competition

- Let the salesperson know you are talking to their competitors.

- Have business cards from their nearest rival on display during the discussion.

- Mention the competition's salesperson by name as if you have already established a close business relationship with them.

- If the car has an equivalent model in another brand, discuss it with them to let them know you are an informed buyer.

Play tough—be prepared not to buy

Before you walk onto the car lot, make a prior decision not to buy unless you get a certain price. By taking this step you will have more confidence and will be able to look them in the eye while saying, 'If I can't buy it for $x, I can't buy it.' Notice the use of the words 'can't buy it' rather than 'won't buy it'. As mentioned before, most car salespeople are very competitive and you need to ensure that when you negotiate with them you do not turn the exercise into a personal challenge. If you inadvertently succeed in stirring up an ego-based challenge they may just be prepared to lose the sale to beat you at your own game.

Use 'time' as your most powerful weapon

Car salespeople use time to generate sales with such monotonous regularity that usually you are not even aware that you are falling for it. For example, special prices that 'end at 12 midday Sunday' is a common way in which time is used to panic people into buying now or risk missing a bargain. However, you too can use time to bluff salespeople.

> Customer: 'I have until Monday to get some money that has fallen due from an investment back into a term investment. At the moment, the money is burning a hole in my pocket which is why I am looking at this car. If you can get the price down to $x by Monday I'll buy it from you. If you can't, don't worry, I understand you can't work miracles. I'll just do the sensible thing and reinvest my money instead of buying this car.'

Having delivered the above soliloquy, make an excuse to leave immediately as you hand them your telephone number 'just in case they can get the price down'. Unless they have completely given up, the salesperson will probably ring you well before Monday with a price somewhere between what you have asked for and what they have offered before. It is very important at this time that you do not speak to them personally. Have someone else take your calls before Monday to keep you away from the salesperson, or vet your calls through your answering machine if you have one.

On Monday, call them mid-afternoon to get their verdict. Remember, by then they believe you have only a couple of hours before you must make your decision—the pressure on them is now enormous if they really want the sale! All of this may sound sneaky but as we have discussed, they will not hesitate to use their own tricks of the trade on you!

Whether you are buying a car, a house or a new outfit, the above rules apply. Do your research, know the seller's competitors and, above all, be prepared to walk out without buying on the day.

CHECKLIST—Conflict resolution skills

❑ I will avoid using the four most common ineffective styles of conflict resolution.

❑ I understand the win-win process and the importance of examining everyone's interests rather than their positions.

❑ I understand how to manage my emotional levels when discussion becomes heated.

❑ I understand how to deal with the emotional outbursts of others.

CHECKLIST—Negotiation skills

❑ I understand the need to know my adversary.

❑ I understand how to apply the powerful tool of time and how not to let others use time to my disadvantage.

❑ I understand the importance of being prepared not to buy on the day.

Chapter 5

Maintaining close relationships with your partner and friends

The aims of this chapter are to:

◆ examine why shared values and interests are important to the well-being of relationships; and

◆ examine ways of building shared values and interests to maintain healthy relationships.

The importance of shared values

An excellent example of the power of shared values and interests occurs when people become stuck in a lift together at work. Regardless of their normal status in the organisation, the Chairman of the Board, the junior personal assistant and the bike courier will all find themselves chatting away given sufficient time trapped in the lift. Their 'shared interest' is their present situation, and how long it will be before they are rescued. Initially the conversation may centre around when they are likely to be released but, given sufficient time, it is likely that they will begin to explore other interests such as their favourite TV program or the football teams they follow.

Having values and interests in common is important to our social well-being, and to the health of our relationships with our friends and family. Over the following pages, we will look at how shared values help to keep people together. This chapter looks at how you can ensure that you continue to build shared values and interests into your special relationship with your spouse or partner.

Shared values in the workforce

Have you ever noticed how the people you were once close to at work no longer seem so important to you after they have left the organisation? Even if you arrange a social reunion with them a year later, you essentially find yourselves focusing on topics related to your past work together. Your shared values and interests were the work itself, the sharing of challenges with peers, observing the way your organisation was performing and, of course, organisation gossip! However, once people leave an organisation they also leave its values, and the motivation to keep in regular contact with former work colleagues typically diminishes over time.

In large organisations, managers invest heavily in promoting employee bonding through shared interests and goals. They have learnt that the company Christmas party, the footy tipping contests and residential management courses all contribute to high morale which in turn assists to build a cohesive, happy workforce. In fact, research into organisation effectiveness repeatedly demonstrates that where a workforce has shared interests it will typically outperform that of a rival's where the sense of belonging to a team is low or absent.

In recent times, a number of more enlightened employers have extended their work-based concerns about employees' morale to include 'Employer Assisted Programs' (EAPs). A typical EAP includes free counselling for the employee and even for family members where relationships are going off the rails due to work-related stress, substance abuse or problems at school involving their children. Apart from the moral or ethical imperatives for looking after employees, such schemes reinforce the feelings of belonging to an organisation where concern for staff is entrenched.

Once you have retired, however, most morale-building activities are left up to one person—YOU! If you are fortunate enough to be in a caring relationship then you are off to a good start. However, as the *Retire 200* research showed, this is not always the case. Before retiring, it is very easy for busy working couples to go about their lives in a constant state of chaos. Trying to find a balance between working, attending to family responsibilities and leisure becomes a major challenge. As such hectic lifestyles can go on for many years, it is not surprising that couples can arrive at retirement having grown apart and without even being aware that it has happened. Now suddenly they have each other's undivided attention. What were seemingly minor issues when submerged in the business of day-to-day life may now become significant problems in retirement when life's work-related distractions have disappeared.

Shared values in personal relationships

'The kids had long grown up and left home. I worked only three days a week and had become involved in volunteer work with my club. During this time, my husband continued to work long hours. On the first Monday morning of his retirement, I looked at him sitting in the loungeroom reading the paper. "This feels strange," I thought. "I'm not sure I like this!"'

On retirement, you are thrown together overnight. Some of the interests that you once shared may have ended years ago. The struggle to pay off the mortgage is over, and the kids have grown up and left home. You may even find that over the years, one of you has changed your political allegiance. Consequently, it is quite common for recently retired couples to experience a wide range of emotions as they adjust to their new lifestyle together. Even in stable, happy relationships one partner may find themselves resenting the other's intrusion into time they previously regarded as their own.

It is important to ensure there are a number of values or interests that you and your partner share in common and which help to keep relationships meaningful. Such commonalities may be your children, your religious or political beliefs, a club or sport, shared values regarding what comprises right and wrong and, of course, mutual admiration, respect and love.

'As soon as I retired we put our plan into action. We bought a caravan and took off. It may not seem very original but it was great fun—both the planning and actually doing it! We will go again next year for sure.'

People strive to create interesting and shared goals together by planning holiday trips. Of course, the trip itself contains intrinsic pleasures, but it is the joint processes of planning and communicating with each other that also provide much of the pleasure.

Building shared values with your partner

The 180° check

As you may be aware, a common practice of many organisations when assessing the performance of employees is to take them through what is called a 360° feedback; this process involves the employee gaining feedback from their manager, their peers, and their direct reports. Consequently, while an employee may honestly believe they are performing well across a range of areas, their manager, peers and reports may have an entirely different view. It can be a painful experience to discover that others regard you as deficient in an area where you thought you were performing well!

The table below contains a 180° check for the use of you and your partner. It essentially contains the components of the 360° feedback format minus the manager's and the direct reports sections. It is designed to help you verify whether you and your partner (or friends) have similar perceptions about each other and where your areas of commonality of attitude and opinion lie.

The process works by completing the table *as you see yourself* and simultaneously having your friend or partner complete the table *as they see you*. The process is then repeated for your partner. When you have finished, compare your impressions of yourself with your partner's impressions of you, and have them do the same. (You can photocopy the blank questionnaire in the Appendices for extra 180° forms.)

If you do not like what you learn from the 180° check, take the bad news with dignity and maturity—make a decision to try to improve. Try not to regress into childhood by yelling, screaming, pouting, and denial! Instead, rejoice in your shared values and take remedial action if you find that differing values are placing a strain on the relationship.

The 180° Check

Area	Terrible, ghastly	Needs to improve	Fair to average	Quite good	A saint
My general planning ability					
My money management					
My consideration for my partner's feelings					
My consideration for my partner's needs for autonomy and time alone					
My consideration for my partner's need for joint activities with me					
The degree to which I accept responsibility for duties around the home					
The level of empathy I demonstrate when my partner is not well or is sad					
The degree to which I am prepared to attend an outing I will dislike but which I know my partner will enjoy					
The number of little things I do that say 'I love you'					

Area	Terrible, ghastly	Needs to improve	Fair to average	Quite good	A saint
The level of respect I show for my partner's wishes and opinions					
The manner in which I speak to my partner at home					
The manner in which I speak to my partner in public					
My preparedness to be welcoming and polite to friends of my partner that I do not like					
The effort I make to be pleasant when I am in a bad mood or upset					
The level of responsibility I take for communicating with our children and grandchildren					
My preparedness to answer the telephone when neither of us feels like it					
The level to which we share driving on a long trip					
My sense of humour					
Other?					
Other?					

Decision-making and Task-allocation matrix

If the 180° check did not cause World War III in your household and you believe that further assessment of your relationship can improve its overall functioning, then try the decision-making and task-allocation matrix (DMTA).

The DMTA matrix has five cells. You make a list of the decisions and tasks you typically share or make with your partner, then you both separately assign each decision or task to what you believe *should be* the correct cell. The following are some areas of responsibilities to start you off—you can add some more of your own. (There is another copy of the DMTA in the Appendices.)

1. Deciding where to go for holidays.

2. Setting the weekly/monthly budget.

3. What colour to paint the house.

4. Whether to move house or not.

5. What price and style of house to purchase.

6. Who looks after the tax returns.

7. Who balances the budget.

8. Who looks after the savings program.

9. Who manages the investments.

10. Who pays the bills.

11. Who makes decisions on maintenance, e.g. repairing versus buying a new hot water system.

12. Who decides whether to buy new appliances, e.g. the latest TV.

13. Who vacuums the house.

14. Who cleans the toilets.

15. Who decides what you will do today.

16. Who decides who you will invite around for dinner.

17. Who decides how you will maintain your health.

CELL A: 100%

(These tasks/decisions are completely mine) e.g. paying the bills

_____

_____

_____

_____

_____

_____

_____

CELL B: 50–50%

(These tasks/decisions are discussed together and voted on) e.g. where you go for holidays

_____

_____

_____

_____

_____

_____

CELL C: 75–25%

(These tasks/decisions are discussed together but if you do not agree, your partner is the decision maker) e.g. what colour to paint the lounge-room

CELL D: 75–25%
(These tasks/decisions are discussed together but if you do not agree, you are the decision maker) e.g. what brand of television set to buy

_____

_____

_____

_____

_____

_____

_____

CELL E: 100%
(These tasks/decisions are completely your partner's) e.g. who looks after the tax returns

_____

_____

_____

_____

_____

_____

_____

Once you have both completed the DMTAs, sit down together (preferably without sharp objects nearby) and discuss your areas of agreement and areas of difference. Ask yourselves the following questions:

- ◆ Are you both happy with these arrangements?
- ◆ Do they expose either of you to risk should one of you become incapacitated or die?
- ◆ Is the distribution of tasks fair given that you are both now retired?
- ◆ What would you like to do differently?
- ◆ What are you going to do about the areas in which you both agree there should be change?

CHECKLIST

❑ I/we will think about, and discuss, ways of building closer relationships where this is required.

❑ I/we will complete the 180° check and discuss areas where our perceptions differ

❑ I/we will complete the DMTA and discuss areas where there is conflict regarding our distribution of responsibilities.

Chapter 6

Contributing and belonging

The aims of this chapter are to:

◆ examine why you need to continue to 'belong' to society when you are retired;

◆ examine ways in which the participants in the *Retire 200* project contributed to their community; and

◆ examine ways in which you can become involved in the community and with others.

Why belonging is important

As you would imagine, your need to belong commenced immediately after you were born. As a baby you quickly developed attachments with the one or two adults who, in most cases, were your parents. This instinctive two-way attachment developed further as the baby 'rewarded' the parents with positive responses such as smiles, happy gestures and baby gurgles. The parents responded with smiles, picking the baby up and cuddling it, contributing baby talk of their own and, of course, providing food. Apart from the mutual pleasures of each other's company, both babies and their parents seek each other's comfort when either is anxious or in danger.

Belonging as adults—genetic selection

There is little doubt that the first human beings, like their animal counterparts, found it necessary to group together to survive the rigours of living in a dangerous environment. Humans who did not group together were left exposed to a number of potentially fatal risks:

◆ Those who preferred to live as individuals or in very small groups were less able to provide sufficient food and safe shelter.

◆ Those who preferred to live alone ran the risk of ending up on the dinner plates of wild animals or other humans.

◆ Those who preferred to live in small groups lacked a wide pool of available mates and consequently reduced their opportunity to breed and to continue their genetic lines.

We can therefore be reasonably sure that the humans who survived through these primitive ages did so because of their preference for affiliating with other humans.

Affiliation

Support and assistance

Today people continue to group together for support and assistance. Formal structures such as governments and local councils are needed to provide health, policing and other community requirements. You also need the company of others so that you can fulfil your desire to feel that you are an important part of your society and community. The strength of the need to belong is borne out by the fact that there are very few genuine voluntary hermits in the world. In the main, people who are isolated from their community tend to be marginalised due to psychological or psychiatric disorders, or have become isolated due to poverty, illness or substance-related problems such as alcoholism.

Fear reduction

After World War II, many psychologists were at a loss to explain how it was that apparently normal human beings could have inflicted the pain and misery that took place in the Nazi concentration camps. In an attempt to answer this disturbing question, a number of experiments were conducted in the 1950s and 1960s. During the experiments, the behaviour of the participants was closely monitored as they were subjected to extreme levels of stress and coercion. In some cases those taking part in the experiments were told to give others severe electric shocks during which time the 'victims' screamed in apparent agony and terror. Later, it would be revealed to those inflicting the shocks that the victims were professional actors and that in fact, no electric shocks had been delivered.

One of the findings of these studies concerned the ways in which participants sought to reduce their fear during the experiments. While those designated as the 'shockers' had to wait their turn, they were given the opportunity to wait *alone* in a room at the university with comfortable chairs and magazines or to wait *together* in an uncomfortable waiting room. The higher their level of fear, the more likely it was that they chose to be together even though it meant waiting in the less comfortable room.

Note: If you have been asking yourself how such experiments could be allowed, the answer is that today they would not be. Experiments which put the psychological well-being of those involved at risk would simply not be allowed.

In retirement, our needs for fear reduction through affiliation usually centre around fears about:

◆ your health and how you will be cared for if you become ill;

◆ whether your finances will be sufficient to support yourself comfortably into old age; and

◆ whether you will be lonely.

Social comparison

Most people like to know how they are performing relative to the rest of society. Social comparison does not just relate to how well you are doing financially or how new your car is compared to that of your neighbour's. People also like to rate themselves against others in terms of intelligence and attractiveness. When you compare favourably with those around you, you feel reassured. This explains why we feel most comfortable when we are mixing with people who are similar in age, educational level and financial status. On the other hand, if you find yourself in an environment where most of your neighbours are wealthier, better educated and appear to be participating in a more enjoyable, vibrant lifestyle, then you are likely to become disillusioned and dissatisfied.

The desire for community involvement

'You need to be involved in the community.'

'Find a way of being of value to your community—you will also find rewarding relationships.'

'Do things you are interested in and ensure you understand issues outside your own four walls.'

A number of people in the *Retire 200* program were keen to ensure that they played an active role in their community for two main reasons:

◆ Some were concerned that without involvement in their community they would become cut off from the mainstream of life. For these people 'community' sometimes referred to the community of their immediate neighbourhood or even of their local church. For others, it referred to the broader community of their municipality or region.

◆ Some people saw themselves as experienced human resources who could provide valuable input to maintain the 'social health' of the community. For example, some were concerned that local requirements of the aging were met, while others were more concerned about a lack of leisure activities for the youth of their community.

The desire for power

'I was at the top of the company and we employed over 1500 people. You walk out of the door and it is a hell of a shock when you find that they can keep on going without you.'

While this former managing director highlights a common dilemma for retired senior executives, it is not too far removed from us all. No matter what level you have attained as an employee, or in your own business, everyone likes to think that in some way they are indispensable. People want to believe that there are certain vital qualities that only they can bring to an enterprise. It is quite natural, therefore, to feel somewhat wounded when you learn that things are going well in the workplace without you.

Unfortunately, it is when your own self-esteem is taking a hammering that you can unwittingly take your frustration out on those who are closest to you. The immediate effects of diminished self-esteem may include responses ranging from anger to depression and withdrawal. Being the partner of someone in such an emotional state is far from pleasant. Ironically, the partner on the receiving end of the recent retiree's distress is also often adjusting to retirement; for them, the problem is compounded as they deal with their partner's emotional problems and their own adjustment to retirement.

The desire for a purpose in life

> 'I was the principal of the local primary school. I loved my job and I loved the children. I can still hear the school bell chiming from where we live and my husband, who hated his job, can't understand why this sometimes reduces me to tears.'

We all need to be needed. If your partner is going through the 'just retired blues' there is much you can do to help them. The simple act of encouraging them to talk about their feelings, and then listening carefully, is worth its weight in gold. Where missing work develops into depression, professional assistance is recommended. Post-retirement depression and strategies for reducing it are discussed in more detail in Chapter 10.

Ways to contribute and belong

Voluntary work

> 'Look for voluntary work.'

> 'Get out into the community and do work for others in which money does not change hands.'

'Volunteering is great—it gives purpose to life. Things that involve people make you feel good.'

'There is no tax on helping others.'

'Involve yourself in voluntary work—it has so much to offer and is so satisfying.'

'Keep as active as possible—do something useful for yourself and for others if possible.'

If there was one common sentiment expressed about voluntary work, it was 'I always get more out of it than I put into it.' The range of voluntary positions that people held was diverse. Some people were involved in helping with meals-on-wheels, working with their church, recording talking books for the blind, working on committees or serving in the shops of organisations such as Oxfam. Others worked for charitable organisations, visited the terminally ill, arranged local town clean-ups or helped newcomers learn English. There were also those who became involved by donating their time to arts councils or other special interest bodies.

Volunteers often spoke about their initial introduction to voluntary work. Many reported that they had offered to 'help out for a while' only to find themselves still involved years later. However, most agreed that it is not *who* you choose to help that is important; it is the sense of achievement from making a worthwhile contribution that provides the real rewards.

One man who regularly visits those suffering from terminal illness described how he was introduced to voluntary work.

'A friend of mine was diagnosed with cancer. He was in hospital for nearly a year before he died. I would visit him at least weekly and the experience was always the same. As I would travel in the lift to his ward, I would feel a sense of apprehension come over me. What was I going to talk about that would help him feel better? After a few visits it dawned on me that what I actually said did not really matter. It was far more important just to be there for him and to provide human contact.

'As I would leave him at the end of each visit, I would feel an inner strength and peace. The paradox was that I seemed to be gaining strength and comfort from him!'

As this volunteer visited his friend he became aware of other patients in the ward who appeared to have few if any visitors and he would often find himself speaking with them too. Some time after his friend died he decided to seek out lonely terminally ill patients and to visit them on a regular basis.

Helping adult children

'I believe you need to have a function in your family that adds to their net worth.'

This comment highlights the importance of keeping close to your family. They need you to help out in their busy lives, and you need them and the fulfilment that can be gained from helping them. Many retirees report that being able to help their adult children either financially or through providing services such as baby-sitting is one of the major pleasures in their lives.

Joining

'When you are retired you find you have a need for an identity or a peer group to belong to.'

There are a number of groups catering for retired people. Some retirees attend classes, while others lecture or run courses in an area in which they possess skills. Consequently, people attending colleges, whether as students or lecturers, are able to mix with others of similar interests while gaining intellectual stimulation.

'You need to meet with people similar to yourself, otherwise you feel isolated from society.'

Groups based on membership of people with similar interests include retired employees' associations and Rotary and Lions clubs.

Women's clubs and associations

'Women should take up a hobby in their fifties and join/form a group of women they see outside work. If you have that group and then lose your husband or your job, they are still there for you.'

It would be going out on a controversial limb to state that women are more supportive of each other than are men. However, during interactions with the research participants it was common to encounter members of women's groups who had been together for many years and who continued to offer each other company and support. One particular group comprised fifteen teachers and ex-teachers who met for lunch on a monthly basis. They gave and received emotional support from each other at these meetings and intended to maintain the group for the rest of their lives.

Successful women's groups generally have two key elements in common:

◆ The women had some form of shared interest ranging from membership of the same previous occupation to sharing an interest, e.g. oil painting or a craft. In rural areas, commonality was sometimes as basic as the remoteness of the region in which they lived.

◆ In each group there were invariably one or two women whose commitment and organisational abilities ensured that the group met regularly, that birthday lists were maintained and that meeting venues were booked.

The members of such groups typically felt that membership of a women's group was so worthwhile that women who could not find a group to join should consider establishing one of their own.

Getting involved—it takes effort!

'You need the willingness to go out and meet people—to socialise.'

Sometimes when you are lonely or feeling down, the last thing you feel like doing is making the effort to move into a new environment and start socialising. This can be particularly difficult for those who have lost their partner and who are venturing out by themselves at a time when they feel especially vulnerable. If you have lost your partner, groups such as Solace (a self-help group for those who have lost a partner through death) can be a safe starting place where everyone else in the room is in the same situation.

CHECKLIST

❑ I understand the motivators for affiliation.

❑ I have read the feedback from the participants in the *Retire 200* program.

❑ I will consider my own needs to take part in community work or to join a service organisation.

SECTION III:

Enjoying a long, happy retirement

The research findings indicated that where people exercise regularly, maintain a healthy diet and have a medical check-up at least annually, they are less likely to find themselves suffering from anxiety, stress and depression. Of course, it really should not need the *Retire 200* study to convince anyone of the need to take responsibility for their health. There is more than enough evidence confronting us daily in the media to reinforce the benefits of activities designed to maintain good health.

Years ago the links between smoking and health were less well known, at least to the general public. About the worst information people were given about smoking was that it would stunt your growth! Around that time our next door neighbour was smoking 80 cigarettes a day. He had tried on a number of occasions to give up smoking because of the expense involved, however nothing seemed to work. One day during a visit to his doctor to discuss some uncomfortable sensations in his left leg he was told that if he did not immediately cease smoking he was in danger of losing the leg. Not wanting to believe that this could be true, our neighbour kept on smoking at the same rate. A year later his leg was amputated. Undeterred, he continued to smoke. Finally, he was warned, 'Cease smoking immediately, the same problem is occurring in your other leg.' This time he stopped; it was now easy—he was finally motivated!

For those of you who are making the effort to regularly maintain your health it may seem strange that others do not. Surely, if people know that there are clear benefits to exercising, having a healthy diet and having a regular medical check-up, why are they not *all* participating?

The simple answer is that for many of us, it just gets down to our personal levels of motivation. The time involved or the discomfort from exercising may just not seem to be worth the effort. Here are some possible explanations for this behaviour:

Exercise: For those who are not interested in sport, or who prefer to engage in sedentary pursuits such as reading or using computers, exercise may be boring or at odds with what they really want to do. A comfortable chair and a good book can simply be too tempting for some people. Unfortunately this situation is not helped by the fact that the less we do physically, the less we want to do.

Diet: Unhealthy food is often tempting because of the short-term reward versus long-term deficit response. This simply means that the tempting rich food we eat now rewards the taste buds immediately, while the elevated cholesterol and additional kilograms we gain do not affect us for some time. The same reasoning explains why it is that some of us continue to drink too much alcohol although we may suffer appalling hangovers the next day. The immediate pleasure gained from drinking the alcohol is too far removed in time from the hangover to motivate us to cut down!

Check-ups: The reasons we may have for not taking annual medical examinations can be more complex. Some people have a real fear that if they present for a check-up, the doctor may discover something wrong. For example, many women report that as the time approaches for their regular mammogram they find themselves becoming increasingly anxious. Following the mammogram their anxiety may reach very high levels as they wait for the results to come through. Of course, we all know at a logical level that early detection is an important factor in improving outcomes in these cases. However, at an emotional level, denial and procrastination are sometimes easier options. A work colleague died some years ago simply because he kept putting off a colonoscopy until his bowel cancer had progressed too far. It is quite likely that he would have survived had he been screened even a year earlier.

For those who contribute to a healthy lifestyle through regular exercise, a balanced diet and annual check-ups this section of the book may not be required reading. However, the statistics indicate that you are very much in the minority. The trouble is that people are very skilled at believing what they want to believe. In the *Retire 200* program participants' pro-active health habits were examined. It was quite common when asking someone if they looked after their diet to have them cite their healthy practice of, say, eating fresh fruit, low fat soy milk and low fat yoghurt for breakfast each morning. Unfortunately, the same person would conveniently forget the four strong coffees, the cake at morning tea and the high fat, low fibre food they regularly consumed each night. It's not that we deliberately lie about our diets, it's just that we like to remember the reassuring, good things we do while trying to forget the habits we know impact adversely on our health.

The following chapters on physical health will therefore help motivate you to maintain your good health by:

- identifying the importance of exercise along with some ways of making it more interesting;
- examining the importance of a good, well-balanced diet together with suggestions for improving it; and
- discussing the importance of having a regular medical check-up as you get older.

Chapter 7

Regular exercise

The aims of this chapter are to:

◆ identify the benefits of engaging in regular, balanced exercise;

◆ explore the types of exercise that are important to the maintenance of good health; and

◆ examine ways of making exercise more interesting for those of us who are not naturally inclined towards physical activity.

Exercise—why do it?

Suddenly discovering that exercise is important to their continued good health and longevity will not usually convert a sedentary slob into a fit, energetic exerciser. However, when people discover that exercise may help make life more fulfilling and more enjoyable, then some may start to look a little closer. The following are some compelling reasons in favour of exercising.

Exercise helps you relax

After a reasonable amount of exercise your body produces chemicals known as neurotransmitters. Among these are endorphins, which produce the sensation of well-being sometimes described by athletes as the 'endorphin rush'. The result is a feeling of relaxation and an improved state of mind. In fact, those who exercise regularly say that they become quite grumpy if they are forced to miss their endorphin rush due to a cold or for some other reason that temporarily prevents exercising.

Exercise helps build self-esteem

Making the effort to get fit improves your self-esteem because you no longer view yourself as a helpless blob at the mercy of a sedentary lifestyle. Even a brisk fifteen-minute walk daily will start to turn around your levels of fitness. The resulting feeling of well-being and the sense of taking control of your own destiny will improve your self-esteem.

Exercise reduces the likelihood of developing certain medical conditions

Participating in regular exercise has been linked to a reduction in the incidence of high cholesterol levels, heart disease, stroke, blood pressure, osteoporosis, cancers and diabetes just to mention a few. These facts may surprise you:

- Recent research indicates that exercise can make a significant contribution to improved health in those suffering from non-insulin-dependent diabetes.

- Exercise can assist in the prevention of some cancers by lowering dietary fats, which in turn may also lower oestrogen—high oestrogen production has been linked to the incidence of cancer of the endometrium. Also, there is medical evidence to suggest that overweight people have a heightened risk of contracting some cancers. Finally, exercise reduces the incidence of constipation, which is correlated with an increased incidence of colon cancer.

- It has been established that the right combination of load-bearing exercises can assist in building bone density. This in turn reduces the likelihood of fracture due to weakened bones.

- It can be tempting to stop exercising due to the pain of osteoarthritis. However, doing this can result in compounding the problem because muscles become weaker through the reduced exercise, which in turn places more strain on the joints, causing further degeneration of the cartilage necessary for smooth, painless movement of the joints. Where arthritis is present, sufferers usually need to ensure that their exercise is non-impact (for example, swimming). It is important that arthritis sufferers check with their doctor regarding the amount and frequency of their exercise program.

◆ Recent findings indicate that activity in the form of aerobic exercise contributes to a decrease in low-density lipoprotein cholesterol (which is associated with hardening of the arteries) and an increase in high-density lipoprotein cholesterol (the so-called 'good cholesterol').

If you exercise, you are more likely to eat healthy food and keep your weight under control

If you schedule time for exercise, pay out money for gym classes or purchase exercise gear to exercise regularly you will also find that you are less prepared to undo all your good work with indiscriminate eating. Psychologists refer to this situation as avoiding cognitive dissonance, that is, avoiding those behaviours that conflict with your beliefs.

Life is better!

If you feel healthier, have more energy, have higher self-esteem and generally feel fit then life is more enjoyable. Exercise is linked to all of these benefits.

Women and exercise

A group of 218 women were asked why they exercised. They answered:

I want to improve my fitness
I like to get exercise
I like the company
I like to have fun
I like the social aspects
I want to release tension
I like to get out of the house
I like the rewards
I want to learn new things

I want to be physically fit
I like the activity
I like the exercise instructors
I like being part of a group
I want to stay in shape
I like to meet new friends
I like the challenge
I like to have something to do
I want to be with my friends

I like to do something I am good at

I like to travel to the exercise sessions

I like to feel important

I want to get rid of energy

My family and friends want me to exercise

I want to be noticed for what I do

I want to be popular

As you can see, there are many more reasons for exercising than just maintaining your health. For many people, an exercise regime forms a significant part of their social life.

How to begin

If you are about to commence or increase your exercise program, it is wise to play safe and have a medical examination first. When you see your doctor, mention that your reason for visiting is to be assessed for suitability for exercise, so that they know where to focus their attention. They may look for evidence of any of the following complaints:

Heart condition. They may ask about the type of heartbeats that you experience after exercise—are they slow or fast? Do they appear to be irregular? Do you experience any chest pain during exercising? How quickly does your heart rate return to your normal rate after exercising?

Malignancies or conditions such as diabetes. They may ask if you have experienced dizziness or loss of consciousness, or if you have had unexplainable falls during the last few months. They may also ask about any unusual weight loss you have experienced recently.

Joint or bone conditions such as arthritis. Certain types of physical activity may adversely affect these conditions, so the doctor may ask if you experience pains in your legs after walking or whether any of your joints become swollen or cause you pain after exercise.

Circulatory problems. You may be asked if you encounter any calf pain when you exercise, which may indicate that the arteries in your leg are clogged with cholesterol thus restricting your exercise potential.

Components of a good exercise program

The aim of the medical examination is not to try to find reasons to prevent you from exercising. Rather it is to clear the way for you to exercise with confidence, knowing that you are doing the right thing by your body. Even if certain medical conditions are detected during the examination, it is unlikely that exercise will be forbidden. In fact it is more likely that correct exercise will then become even more important to help reduce the symptoms and possibly the progression of the complaint.

Assuming a relevant professional has examined you and no reasons for avoiding certain types of exercise have been identified, your program should include three main components.

Aerobic exercise

Aerobic exercises involve the use of the large muscle groups and include such activities as walking, swimming, skipping, dancing, cycling and rowing. Aerobic exercise helps deliver oxygen to the muscles and is particularly important for maintaining a healthy cardiovascular system. It is also the main type of exercise usually associated with controlled weight loss.

Strength building (anaerobic) exercise

Building strength in the right muscle groups can reduce the likelihood of back injuries. It can also improve your stability, which in turn minimises the chance of falls. Building supporting muscle around the joints and back will likewise provide more skeletal support to keep you upright and mobile. When designing strength building programs you should normally include all of the major muscle groupings, that is, the back, legs, stomach, arms and chest.

Stretching

Warming up and warming down exercises are believed by many people to minimise the risk of injury from using muscles that are not yet ready to go to work. Proper pre- and post-exercise stretching are also believed by many to prevent much of the stiffness that people may experience after heavy exercise. Regardless of the benefits of stretching, most athletes report that they enjoy the sensation of stretching their muscles before and after exercise. Include stretching exercises that cover all the major muscle groups.

When you warm up you need to:

◆ Include aerobic exercises that you start slowly and gradually build up. For example, if you are riding a bike, start by pedalling slowly for a while to allow the muscle groups that you are using to warm up and to get the blood flowing to them.

◆ Once you have warmed-up for about ten minutes, complete some stretching exercises that work on the muscles you intend to use during your exercise. Begin each stretch slowly so that you do not over-stretch the muscle. Hold the stretch for between 10 and 30 seconds. Remember these rules of stretching:

(a) only stretch those muscles that have been included in your warm-up exercises;

(b) stretch gently and slowly; if you start to experience pain, stop stretching that muscle immediately;

(c) remember to breathe during the stretching process; breathing is important to help keep fresh oxygen flowing to the muscles. Many people new to exercise forget to do this. They are becoming so focused on the stretching process that they inadvertently hold their breath, which eventually becomes quite uncomfortable!

Forms of exercise

Exercise does not have to be complicated, expensive or time consuming. The following ideas are ones that you can put into action now.

Walking

All you need is a pair of good quality walking shoes designed to support and cushion your feet from injury. You can start by walking for just a few minutes at a time if you wish. If you are unfit, try walking for a few minutes in the morning and a few minutes in the afternoon. As you become fitter, gradually increase the time you walk each day.

You can improve the quality of your exercise by adding other mini-exercises as you go. You can walk faster, walk up hills (inclines, rather than Mt Everest), swing your arms and carry hand weights (sometimes called 'heavy hands') to build strength in your arms, wrists and upper chest muscles as you walk.

Swimming and other aquatic exercises

Swimming is popular because:

◆ heated pools are found in most suburbs and large towns, meaning that your exercise program can be conducted all through the year in comfort;

◆ it involves very little stress to your joints, bones and muscles; and

◆ it works on building muscle strength as well as providing cardiovascular aerobic exercise, which is beneficial to your heart.

Cycling (outdoors and exercise bikes)

Bike riding is excellent cardiovascular exercise and works on many of the large muscle groups. If you have not ridden a bike for many years, it is wise to start off slowly again. Find a safe place where it does not matter if you wobble around for a while as you get used to the skill of riding. Those returning to bike riding after many years should obviously avoid busy roads and loose surfaces. Falling off a bike onto a hard surface is no fun and can cause some pretty nasty injuries, particularly as we get older. Therefore, if you have any reason to believe that your stability on a bike is questionable, it is probably wiser to use an exercise bike. Some retailers will let you hire an exercise bike on a monthly basis with the option to purchase if you decide to keep going.

Using the stairs

If you look around, opportunities to use stairs are easy to find. The car parks in most large shopping malls are accessible by stairs and the various levels in the shopping centres have stairs as alternatives to the escalators and lifts. Try using them.

Join a gym

Gyms have improved greatly over the last few years—the equipment is better and the staff are more likely to be well trained. However, always ask around before you sign up for a program. In particular, look for evidence that the gym staff are experienced in designing exercise programs for people of your age. Try ringing around a few local physiotherapists and ask if they can recommend a reputable gym in your area.

Gyms can help you stay motivated because:

◆ good gyms are not cheap—outlaying money for membership may help you continue to exercise to justify the cost;

◆ a good gym will keep records of your improving performance—this will help encourage you to continue; and

◆ you will be in the company of others who are also doing their best to get fit—as you look around you will see that not all in the gym are young and beautiful. This should encourage you if your own body shape is less than perfect!

Boredom

Okay—I think I understand you. You want to be fit but you are just not interested in exercise activities. What is more, you may never have been! For you there is a need for special motivation. Do not feel guilty—you have many like-minded colleagues. In fact, the person who finally invents a well-rounded exercise program that sedentary people can enjoy and flock to will become a multi-millionaire overnight! However, until that program comes along there are a number of steps you can take to make exercise more interesting and more fun.

Find an exercise soul mate

Among your friends or acquaintances there is bound to be someone else just like you—someone who knows they should exercise but who so far has not found the motivation to do so. Tell them how you feel about exercise and ask them whether they would like to join you on an exercise program where you could motivate each other. Having an exercise partner will relieve much of the boredom and will provide you with the drive to keep going through sharing a common goal.

The company of groups

If you cannot find an exercise partner or think you would prefer to exercise with a larger group of people, consider joining a walking club or a gym. You will often find notices about walking clubs and other group exercise activities on the noticeboards at gyms or in your local library.

Tell the world

Throw caution to the wind. Tell everyone that you are starting an exercise program so that you deliberately set yourself up for an embarrassing backdown if you quit. Tell people to ask you regularly how your exercise program is going. Use the method adopted by Alcoholics Anonymous — call on your friends if you feel like quitting.

Start off slowly

Try not to let your newfound enthusiasm cause you to overdo things too soon into your program. Start slowly and gradually build up. If you rush things you run the risk of either injuring yourself or becoming so stiff and sore that you will start to believe all those reasons you once had for not exercising!

Encourage yourself—focus on the process, not the end result

One of the most self-defeating behaviours you can indulge in as a new exerciser is to expect rewards such as weight loss, tightened stomach muscles or years off your appearance after only a couple of weeks of activity! Encourage yourself to focus on the process of exercising rather than on the pay-offs—these will not occur until sometime in the future. You are setting yourself up for disappointment if you expect too much too soon. In fact, if weight loss is your primary goal, you may initially be dismayed to notice your weight increase because muscle weighs more than fat.

Look for aesthetically pleasing surroundings

Some people love the environment of the gymnasium with its exercise machines, grunting, sweating people and the aroma of liniment and sweat in the air. For others, that may sound much like a description of Hell! If you are to remain happy and motivated, look for somewhere that is pleasing to *your* senses. This may mean that a gym is not for you, in which case a park or a leafy residential street may comprise a more uplifting environment.

Build variety into your program

Think about ways in which you can introduce variety to your surroundings. This may mean that on some days you drive or catch a bus or train to a different location to walk. Use your imagination to vary your surroundings to meet your own needs.

Don't expect your progress to mirror that of others

People progress through exercise differently due to their individual metabolism or previous levels of fitness. You may find that if you are exercising with a friend, one of you may seem to be getting fit quicker than the other. Try not to become frustrated by this. You will find that some people leap ahead and then reach a plateau where they stay for some time. Others find the going difficult at first and then suddenly find themselves speeding ahead, while others just progress slowly and steadily from the start.

If exercising alone, find ways to entertain yourself

Some people like to exercise as they listen to a portable radio-cassette player. It's a great way to combine exercise and music, or to listen to your favourite radio program. If you decide to do this while walking on the streets, remember to be careful of traffic. It is very easy to become immersed in the music or talkback and not hear nearby traffic.

Reward yourself for attaining milestones

Identify specific goals such as walking the distance to the shopping centre and back in one go. When you achieve a goal, reward yourself, preferably with something that is not fattening! Buy yourself a ticket to a show or to some other event that you will enjoy. As you arrive say to yourself, 'This is my reward for achieving x days of exercise.'

Exercise versus ecology

What do you do when your husband wants to stroll slowly along admiring the wildlife and plants while all you want to do is power walk your way to fitness? One couple found the perfect solution.

Lynne and Ross live in rural Victoria. Lynne enjoys the challenge of a long brisk walk early each morning. The trouble is that while Ross also enjoys a walk, his real interest is in admiring the wildflowers by the roadside. After a number of mutually frustrating walks where neither partner was entirely satisfied with the outcome, they came up with the perfect solution.

Each morning, Lynne sets off for her brisk walk to the picnic area by the lake some kilometres away. Ross then drives their campervan down to the lake and prepares breakfast while he waits for Lynne to arrive.

On Lynne's arrival they sit down together and enjoy breakfast overlooking the lake. Afterwards, Ross sets out on his stroll and Lynne drives the campervan back home.

CHECKLIST

❑ I have had a medical check-up and have been cleared to commence regular exercise.

❑ I have thought about the most enjoyable types of exercise for me.

❑ I have found an exercise partner or group.

❑ I have told people that I have started exercising.

❑ I am building variety into my exercise program so that I am less likely to become de-motivated.

❑ I have now exercised for one week.

❑ I have now exercised for two weeks.

❑ I have now exercised for four weeks.

❑ I have now exercised for three months.

❑ I have now exercised for six months.

❑ I have now exercised for one year.

Chapter 8

A healthy diet

The aims of this chapter are to:

◆ identify the benefits of a healthy versus an unhealthy diet;

◆ identify food groups found in a healthy well-balanced diet; and

◆ discuss easy ways to adapt to a healthy, enjoyable diet.

Balancing your diet

Most people have a fair idea why they should avoid fatty, salty, sugary foods, so providing a litany of reasons for avoiding the wrong food is probably not going to be of much help. Instead, the foods commonly found in a balanced diet are examined.

Vegetables

Eat vegetables steamed, cooked in a microwave, stir-fried or raw to obtain the maximum benefit from them. Boiling will only serve to destroy vitamin content, and frying introduces fat.

Fruit

Fruit is one of those food types that people either love or just find boring. If you are in the latter category, it may be that your definition of fruit revolves around the same old varieties of apples, bananas and oranges that you have eaten since childhood. While these are fine, we also have a wide variety of fruit available practically all year round. Some of the more exotic fruits tend to be a little more expensive, but compared to tinned or processed foods they are still excellent value for money. If you have not been a big fruit eater, try experimenting with some varieties that you do not usually buy.

Protein

When you are selecting your source of protein, ensure that you pick low fat categories. Choose lean meat cuts such as turkey or chicken breasts, fish, lentils, peas, beans or bean curd (tofu).

Dairy foods

Include dairy foods but look for the low fat or no fat varieties of yoghurt, cheese or milk.

Grains

Include wholemeal bread, wholegrain breakfast cereals, pasta, rice or rolled oats.

Water

Drink a minimum of six to eight glasses of water a day. If you are going to be physically active, you will need to drink even more. Be sure to carry water with you if you are going to the gym or on long walks.

Identifying the good and avoiding the bad

Alcohol

Unless you have been living on another planet, you will probably be able to compile a list of many of the terrible calamities that alcohol abuse can bring. 'But wait,' some of you may say, 'I've heard that drinking one or two glasses of wine a day is good for you'. Well yes, you probably did. It appears that having one or two glasses of wine each day is associated with a number of health benefits. The trouble is that many of the people who gleefully trot out the wine-is-good-for-you argument appear to be consuming far more than two glasses of wine a day!

At least part of the basis for excessive alcohol consumption is that most people have had little or no training in how to drink in moderation! In Australia, binge drinking is even reinforced in our culture. A lifelong friend of mine who came to Australia as a teenager was amazed to discover our drinking habits. 'In Europe we drink with our meals,' he said. 'Here you drink to drink.'

It is never too late to learn a few tricks when it comes to drinking alcohol such as:

◆ Think for a second or two before you raise the glass to your lips and ask, 'Why am I drinking this—do I really want a drink now, or am I just thirsty?' If you are thirsty, the last thing you should drink is alcohol. Have a long glass of water. *Then* have a glass of wine or whatever—this time, sip the wine and savour its flavour.

◆ When drinking at dinner, either at home or in restaurants, always have a jug of water close by and drink the water between sips of wine. In this way you are less likely to throw the wine down to quench your thirst. It is preferable to just diluting the wine, because you retain the ability to appreciate its full flavour.

◆ Always have food or nibbles handy as you drink. Having eaten some food before you drink slows down the rate at which the alcohol is absorbed into your bloodstream and helps prevent that light-headed feeling that can accompany the consumption of alcohol on an empty stomach. Avoid salty nibbles that will only make you thirsty.

◆ Refill your glass when it is empty rather than continually retopping it, so that you can more accurately estimate how much you are drinking. Tell waiters and others that you wish to fill your own glass. If this is not possible, use the following method of monitoring your alcohol consumption which is used by an old friend of mine who attends many social functions in his profession:
  • Determine in advance how many drinks you wish to consume.
  • Place the same number of matches in your pocket.
  • As you finish a drink, discard a match.
  • If a waiter tops up a half empty glass break a match in two and discard half the match.
  • When the matches are all gone, you have reached your quota.

Calcium

As most people know, diet plays an important part in the prevention of osteoporosis, with calcium being important for the health of both our muscles and bones. If we do not consume enough calcium, other parts of our body that require it will raid it from our bones.

Some years ago osteoporosis was regarded as a problem faced only by women. However, increasingly sedentary lifestyles are now resulting in osteoporosis becoming a problem for men too. Unfortunately, not a lot of foods contain calcium and other substances such as alcohol, salt, caffeine and nicotine actually reduce its effectiveness in the body. To increase your calcium intake:

◆ eat tinned or fresh salmon on sandwiches—salmon is an excellent source of calcium;

◆ eat fish instead of meat one or two nights a week;

◆ use low fat yoghurt instead of sour cream;

◆ use low fat milk as a drink to replace soft drinks or coffee; and

◆ replace meat with tofu (soy bean curd) for one meal a week; adding some low salt soy sauce will reduce the blandness of the tofu.

Fat

Fat is usually discussed under three categories:

◆ **Saturated fats.** Saturated fats contribute to high cholesterol levels. They occur in animal fats and are also found in some processed foods such as biscuits, chocolate and cakes.

◆ **Monounsaturated fats.** These fats occur naturally in avocados, olives, peanuts and canola oil. They are known to help in reducing 'bad' cholesterol (low-density lipoprotein) without affecting the 'good' cholesterol (high-density lipoprotein).

◆ **Polyunsaturated fats.** These fats are found in game meats such as kangaroo and rabbit, in fish, in a number of nuts and grains and in vegetable oils. The jury appears to be out on the benefits of these fats. On one hand, research has shown that replacing saturated fats with polyunsaturated fats reduces the incidence of heart disease. However, other studies have indicated that high intakes of polyunsaturated fats may elevate the risk of cancer.

All fats, whether beneficial to your cholesterol levels or not, contain similar levels of calories or kilojoules. Some suggestions for reducing the fat content of your daily diet include:

◆ Eat wholemeal toast at breakfast instead of muffins or croissants, as these usually have a high oil content.

◆ Avoid sausages. A friend of mine used to refer to sausages as 'mystery bags', however, there is no mystery—they are usually very fatty, very salty and often contain preservatives to stop the meat going bad.

◆ Reduce your butter and margarine intake. Low fat mayonnaise spread on one piece of bread in a sandwich is surprisingly pleasant and will help you gradually wean yourself off fatty spreads.

◆ When buying dairy foods, get into the habit of selecting low fat varieties of milk, cheese and yoghurt. Plain low fat yoghurt can be substituted for sour cream on baked potatoes.

◆ When you are selecting meats, pick lean cuts such as chicken breasts, veal, fillet steak or rabbit. In the case of poultry, always remove the skin as it contains a lot of fat.

◆ Replace meat with seafood from time to time. Seafood can be steamed, grilled, cooked in the microwave or barbecued in foil. Some naturally oily fish such as mullet can be grilled on the barbecue.

◆ When making salads use low-fat dressings. Rather than just pouring large quantities of dressing over the salad, try adding a small amount and then tossing the salad. If it still needs more dressing, add a small quantity and toss again.

◆ Use good quality oil sprays to coat frying pans rather than pouring in oil that will be absorbed by the food you are cooking.

◆ After a main meal, consider serving a platter of fresh fruit instead of fatty desserts or cheeses.

Fibre

Having sufficient dietary fibre appears to be one of the factors associated with a lowered incidence of bowel cancer. Fibre also helps reduce the incidence of other bowel complaints such as constipation, diverticulitis, haemorrhoids and irritable bowel syndrome. A diet with a reasonable level of natural fibre will also help create the feeling of having had enough to eat. To increase fibre in your daily diet:

- eat fresh fruit and vegetables;
- eat steamed, baked or microwaved potatoes;
- include fibre in your breakfast in the form of porridge (rolled oats) or wholegrain cereals;
- include legumes such as baked beans in your diet; and
- replace meat (which has *no* fibre) with vegetables one or more days a week.

Salt

Research in recent times has produced a number of conflicting results concerning the deleterious effects of salt on health. What is generally acknowledged, however, is that lowering the amount of salt one consumes can reduce high blood pressure. This fact alone provides sufficient justification for reducing salt in your diet.

You will find that just a few days after reducing salty foods your desire for salt will decrease. You will actually start to taste the food itself and may eventually prefer your food without it. You will also find that you become more aware of existing salt in foods. For example, it is only after significantly reducing salt intake that people begin to notice how salty some commercial breads are. To reduce your salt intake:

- Cook your vegetables in a microwave oven, or steam them, instead of boiling them. The natural flavours and salts will be more noticeable than if you leech everything out in a large amount of water. If you must boil vegetables, use as little water as possible.
- Avoid processed meats such as salami where possible. They are usually highly salted and are also very fatty.

◆ Aim to stop adding salt when cooking. It is only a habit and after a short while you will start to notice the true flavours of the food. Try reducing the amount of salt you add to cooking over a period of four weeks until you are adding no salt at all.

◆ When you are buying food products, check to see if they have a low salt version. Many products come in unsalted or low salt versions. Get into the habit of buying them; you will adjust to them very soon.

◆ Use herbs or lemon juice to season food instead of salt.

Sugar

Like salt, sugar has been the subject of conflicting reports concerning its effects on the body. The most definite area of concern, however, is dental decay. Sugar does cause tooth decay which, apart from the pain and inconvenience, is costly to rectify. Sugar can also be a silent partner in the cause of obesity as it is often used to improve the flavour of processed foods that are high in fat. To reduce your sugar intake:

◆ Reduce the amount of sugar you add to your tea and coffee until you are adding none at all. As in the case of salt, you will soon find that you become used to not adding sugar and will soon not miss it.

◆ Add lemon to water and drink it to replace soft drinks that are usually high in sugar.

◆ Eat fresh fruit instead of canned fruit products that usually have a high sugar content. If you are buying canned fruit or fruit juice, select the unsweetened version.

CHECKLIST

❑ I will purchase unsweetened varieties of foods where they are available.

❑ I will purchase low fat varieties of dairy foods and soy products.

❑ I will replace frying food with steaming, microwaving and baking.

❑ I will wean myself off excessive salt and sugar.

❑ I will ensure that I alternate alcoholic drinks with water to rehydrate as I drink.

Chapter 9

Medical check-ups—they may save your life!

The aims of this chapter are to:

◆ identify the benefits of having regular medical check-ups; and

◆ list specific medical conditions that can be avoided, alleviated or cured through early intervention.

Check-ups—why have them?

Many years ago, a client of mine died of a heart attack during a vigorous game of tennis. He was only 33 years old. What could have gone wrong? These are some background details that may begin to explain why this tragedy occurred:

◆ he was grossly overweight;

◆ he rarely exercised—a walk up a short flight of stairs would leave him breathless;

◆ he maintained a regular diet of fatty, unhealthy food;

◆ on the day of his tennis match it was over 30°C; and

◆ he had not played tennis since he was 12 years old.

Following my client's death, it was found that he had an advanced heart complaint. A check-up with a doctor would have confirmed this fact and an appropriate regime of remedial exercise and diet would have been recommended.

Check-ups as we age

Daily discoveries through medical research are now commonplace. Many complaints that were thought to be incurable only a few years ago can now be either significantly relieved or, in many instances, cured altogether. It is important to your continued health and well-being to present yourself for a medical check-up at least once a year. The sooner a suspected medical problem is investigated the more likely it is that it can be arrested or cured while it is still in its early stages.

Arthritis and rheumatism

Arthritis is inflammation in a joint, while rheumatism is a more general term referring to inflammation in joints and conditions present in soft tissue and muscle. Rheumatism includes such complaints as sciatica, tendonitis, lumbago and fibrositis. Symptoms may include:

◆ pain in a joint;

◆ the feeling that a joint is 'frozen';

◆ heat or redness around a joint;

◆ stiffness of a joint in the morning; and

◆ weakness.

It is important to see your doctor early if any of these symptoms appear because there are now modern treatments available for all types of arthritis and rheumatism. For example, seeking early treatment of gout (gouty arthritis) is essential because neglect can involve concurrent insidious kidney damage. The pain caused in the joints of areas such as big toes and knees is caused by the crystallisation of uric acid. These crystals can also form in the kidneys, causing serious damage.

Diabetes

The two common types of diabetes are Insulin Dependent Diabetes Mellitus (IDDM), or Type I Diabetes, which is the type most commonly diagnosed during childhood or as a young adult; and Non-Insulin Dependent Diabetes Mellitus (NIDDM), or Type II Diabetes, which typically occurs in mature adults or those who have become overweight through poor diet and insufficient exercise.

Diabetes is one of those complaints that may be present without people realising it. The symptoms may include excessive thirst and urination, irritability, itching or numbness of the feet, weight loss and blurred vision.

People over the age of 60 should have a diabetes test once a year. At age 65 approximately 15 per cent of the population have the complaint, with this statistic increasing as people get older. If diabetes is left untreated it can cause blindness, kidney failure, heart disease and stroke and may result in the amputation of limbs.

Heart disease and stroke

The most common cause of heart disease and heart attack is a blocked coronary artery due to the build-up of fatty deposits on the walls of the arteries. This build-up causes the arteries carrying blood to the heart to block, which in turn causes a heart attack. A regular medical check-up can help detect the early symptoms of heart disease. From there, treatment to reduce the risk of damage to the heart is usually prescribed. The symptoms of a heart attack include:

◆ a squeezing pain or discomfort in the middle of the chest or from behind the breast bone that lasts for more than 10 to 15 minutes; and

◆ pain radiating to the neck, arms or shoulders.

Along with these symptoms may also be:

◆ a feeling of sickness in the stomach; and

◆ shortness of breath or sweating.

Note: If you or anyone else with you experiences these symptoms, get to a hospital immediately. Do not wait for the discomfort to go away—it may be too late.

When you have your annual check-up it is wise to have your blood pressure and cholesterol levels checked, as high levels in either are a risk factor for heart attack and stroke. Following your examination and an assessment of your health and risk factors, your doctor may suggest that you have an Electro-cardiograph (ECG). This test detects irregularities in the pulse, called atrial fibrillation, which is a high risk factor for stroke. Your doctor may also prescribe aspirin or warfarin (anti-coagulants) to thin your blood and reduce your likelihood of having a stroke.

Urinary incontinence

Urinary incontinence is a condition that affects approximately 40 per cent of people over the age of 75. Women suffering from the complaint outnumber men by about seven to one. It is important to seek medical advice because many cases of incontinence can be controlled or cured. If the problem is left too long, sufferers unnecessarily expose themselves to physical discomfort and psychological distress. The four principal types of urinary incontinence are:

◆ 'Urge' incontinence, which occurs where there is the strong, urgent need to urinate resulting in the person not always making it to the toilet in time. This problem often results from the presence of existing medical conditions such as Parkinson's disease, stroke or an irritable bladder.

◆ 'Reflex' incontinence, which usually occurs where there has been a spinal injury causing the failure of the central nervous system to forward information about bladder function to the brain.

◆ 'Overflow' incontinence, which occurs where a weakened bladder muscle or enlarged prostate causes urine to leak from a bladder that has not been properly emptied.

◆ 'Stress' incontinence, which occurs where urine, usually in small amounts, leaks out during sneezing, laughing, coughing or certain types of physical exertion.

Following a medical examination, strategies such as special exercises may be suggested to reduce the discomfort.

Parkinson's disease

Parkinson's disease occurs most commonly in people between the ages of

50 and 75. The four most common symptoms of the condition are:

◆ Tremor: this occurs most often when the limb is relaxed or not in use. The tremor can appear in fingers, wrists and larger limbs.

◆ Bradykinesia: this refers to a range of symptoms including the characteristic lack of facial expression, which can give the sufferer the appearance of not reacting emotionally to an event.

◆ Poverty of movement: movement can also slow down to the extent that voluntary actions are difficult. In some cases movements such as gestures or those requiring fine motor co-ordination are unable to be carried out, for example, using a screwdriver or writing with a pen.

◆ Rigidity: this symptom refers to the 'freezing' caused by a feeling of stiffness in the muscles. It occurs most often when the sufferer initially attempts to start walking or to stand up.

While at present there is no cure for Parkinson's disease, a combination of drugs, exercise and diet can be used to help reduce the symptoms.

Colon and rectal cancers

Cancer of the colon, also known as the large intestine or large bowel, is a major killer. For a number of years now there have been progressive developments in the procedures to detect early cases of colon cancer or pre-cancers. Pre-cancerous growths called polyps can be detected during a colonoscopy, where the walls in the colon are examined through an instrument called a colposcope. Removal of these polyps during their early stages can prevent the cancer progressing.

It is important that people at risk present for a check-up to determine which examination or test they need to undergo for early screening of colon cancer. Certainly all people over 50 should consult their doctor for advice. Where colon cancer has been diagnosed in a near relative, it is usually recommended that people are screened more frequently. Unfortunately, there are often no symptoms of colon cancer until it has progressed significantly.

People over age 50 or who fall into certain high-risk areas also need to be checked for the development of rectal cancer. The rectum is the last

25 centimetres of the large intestine, which stores waste before its expulsion through the anus.

Screening methods for colorectal cancers include colonoscopy, fecal occult blood test, double contrast barium enema and flexible sigmoidoscopy.

Prostate cancer

Prostate cancer occurs mostly in men over the age of 65. Many of those who are diagnosed with prostate cancer in later life end up dying of something else because the typical onset of the disease concurs with other high-risk illnesses such as stroke or heart disease.

Where there is a family history of prostate cancer, examinations should start as early as age 40. The two most common methods of testing for prostate cancer are:

◆ prostate-specific antigen (PSA) measurement, a blood test designed to detect increases in the PSA enzyme in the blood; and

◆ digital rectal examination (DRE), a method of examining the prostate which has been used for many years and involves the doctor manually feeling the prostate gland for irregularities.

Where there is any doubt about a person's risk factors, both methods of examination are usually suggested, because both the PSA and DRE tests may not always differentiate prostate cancer from benign growths or other prostate-related conditions.

Skin cancer

Three common types of skin cancer are:

Basal cell carcinoma (BCC). While BCC is the most commonly occurring form of skin cancer, it appears to be the least dangerous in that it is less likely than other forms of skin cancer to spread to other areas of the body. BCC is typically found on the face, neck and upper parts of the body. It resembles small round or flattened bumps on the skin and can be from pale to red in colour. Some BCC may have blood vessels on their surface area. BCC usually grow slowly, taking months or years to develop. However, this is not a good reason to leave them untreated as over time they may develop into deep ulcers.

Squamous cell carcinoma (SCC). SCCs form over a period of weeks to months. While they are less common than basal cell carcinomas, they are more dangerous because they may spread to other parts of the body to form a secondary cancer or metastasis. Consequently, it is important to treat this type of skin cancer promptly. SCCs have red, scaling areas and tend to bleed easily and ulcerate. They can look like a sore that is not healing.

Melanoma. This is a fast growing skin cancer and is the most dangerous of the three. It can spread quickly to other parts of the body to form secondary cancers. It is important to understand that melanoma is not just found on parts of the body that are usually exposed to the sun. Melanomas can usually be first detected in a changed mole or freckle, or in a new spot in otherwise normal skin. Any change in shape, colour or size of a mole, freckle or spot on the skin should be promptly checked. Melanomas are sometimes described as looking like the map of an island in that they often have an irregular pattern on their border rather than a neat circle.

To avoid the risk of skin cancers:

◆ use broad spectrum, high SPF-rating sunscreens (for example, 30+, on skin that is not protected by clothing;

◆ wear protective clothing and head gear; and

◆ try to avoid the sun during the middle of the day (or later during daylight savings time).

Breast cancer

The present statistics indicate that about one in fourteen women will develop breast cancer. As the incidence of breast cancer increases with age, women over the age of 50 should use a regular mammogram screening process. This will help detect any problems while they are still in the very early stages and where any changes are still so small that they cannot be detected by self-examination. Mammograms provided by Breast-Screen Australia are presently free of charge.

Cervical cancer

Most cases of the most commonly occurring form of cervix cancer can be prevented through detection with regular Pap (Papanicolaou) screens. Where precancerous cervical lesions are detected the survival rate is nearly 100 per cent, provided it is followed up with early and appropriate treatment. The Pap smear test is a simple procedure that is completed by your doctor or their nurse, in most cases at the doctor's rooms.

Lung cancer and emphysema

People with a long history of smoking are at the highest risk of contracting these diseases—a chest X-ray is used to detect the presence of either complaint. Your doctor will advise you how often you should have a chest X-ray based on your medical history and lifestyle.

CHECKLIST

❑ I have a medical check-up at least once a year.
❑ I believe my doctor is conscientious but would be prepared to change doctors if I detected a lack of high quality service.
❑ I comply with my doctor's recommendations when s/he suggests I have screening tests.

SECTION IV:

Maintaining psychological fitness

For some people, retirement signals the culmination of years of careful planning and financial preparation. The details of an extended trip have been finalised and their life's savings have been distributed across a range of investments designed to maximise retirement income for life. The good life is about to begin!

For others, retirement has been forced by either illness, retrenchment or business closure at an age where gaining further full-time employment is unlikely. In these cases, financial plans may not have been completed and retirement may be approached with nagging concerns about how long the money will last.

However, despite our plans or the lack of them transitions from one stage of life to another are rarely without their surprises. Moving from secondary school to university brings its special stresses, as does the transition from life as a university student to being a member of the workforce. Our later transition to retirement after many years of work also brings its challenges. Some of these challenges will have been predicted by us and will cause little or no problems. Other aspects of the transition, however, will find us temporarily unsettled as we discover that some aspects of life in retirement are not quite what we had expected.

Chapters 10 to 13 provide a number of strategies for dealing with the range of emotional issues you may encounter during your adjustment to retirement.

Chapter 10

Anxiety, depression and stress

The aims of this chapter are to help you:

◆ understand why the process of adjusting to retirement can be associated with emotional difficulties such as anxiety, depression and stress;

◆ understand the fundamental differences between anxiety, depression and stress so that you can recognise them should they occur; and

◆ develop a number of strategies for improving emotional well-being.

Causes of anxiety, depression and stress in retirement

In the *Retire 200* program, the degree to which a participant was regarded as being well-adjusted to retirement was determined by assessing their levels of retirement-related stress, anxiety and depression. Where high levels of these were due to retirement-related issues, those participants were regarded as being less well adjusted to retirement than those whose emotional states were within a normal range.

The factors influencing emotional adjustment to retirement were discussed in detail in the Introduction. This is a summary of those factors:

Reason for retirement. Those whose retirement was forced due to retrenchment or ill-health (their own or that of a relative) were more likely to be anxious, depressed and stressed than those who had retired voluntarily.

Age at retirement. Those who retired at age 55 or younger were associated with lower levels of anxiety than those who retired older.

Financial independence. Those who were financially independent had lower levels of anxiety, depression and stress when compared with those who were reliant on government pensions.

Having a purposeful activity. Those who engaged in purposeful activities, that is, activities that result in the production of something or which provide a service to others, of more than five hours per week were significantly less depressed and stressed in retirement than those who were inactive.

Availability of emotional support. Those who could access emotional support from a family member or friend, if required, were less stressed than those without access to such a resource.

Self-promoted health activities. Self-promoted health activities were activities that people initiated to maintain their health. Activities were divided into three categories: engaging in daily exercise, maintaining a healthy diet, and having an annual medical check-up. Those participants who exercised experienced lower levels of stress. Those who attended to their diet were associated with lower levels of depression. Those who attended to all three categories were less depressed than those who attended to just one or two.

Planning for retirement. Those who planned for their retirement, either financially or for lifestyle reasons such as planning to travel or to be active, were less anxious, depressed or stressed than those who did not plan.

Receiving advice about retirement matters. Those who had sought advice before or during retirement were less depressed than those who did not seek advice.

Because everyone has their own ways of coping, their own levels of self-esteem and their own ways of responding to life's events, not everyone will react in the same way to a particular set of circumstances. For example, the *overall* levels of anxiety in those participants in *Retire 200* with a purposeful activity were lower than for those without. However, there also would have been people who scored low on anxiety even though they had *no* purposeful activity. Similarly, while many people on very low fixed incomes found this situation depressing and stressful, some were unperturbed.

Understanding emotional health

Given the significant impact of emotional health on satisfaction with life in retirement, it is important to be equipped with methods for managing anxiety, depression and stress should these ever become a problem. However, before looking at some ideas for dealing with such emotional issues, it is helpful to have a basic understanding of how anxiety, depression and stress differ.

Anxiety

You will often hear the terms anxiety, fear and phobia used interchangeably as if they were the one concept. While they are all related, they impact on people differently and can be triggered by quite different circumstances.

When people are suffering from anxiety, which is sometimes called 'free-floating' anxiety, they typically describe feeling constantly on edge or on the alert, that all is not well, and that something bad is about to happen. Because of their pervasive nature, this group of anxiety-based symptoms is referred to as 'hypervigilance'. Psychologist Edmund Bourne described the focus of these symptoms as being 'internal' rather than 'external'. In other words, anxiety is not usually related to a visible, external threat but is the personal response to nonspecific, unrecognised danger.

At a physiological level, people who are experiencing anxiety will typically report symptoms such as sweating, dryness in the mouth, queasiness and rapid heartbeat.

Fear differs from anxiety in that it is usually focused on a recognisable external threat. For example, if the dog next door has bitten you, it would be natural to experience fear if you later saw it running towards you as you walked down the street. Similarly, a person whose life savings are heavily exposed to a poorly performing investment may fear losing their financial independence during an unexpected downturn in the economy.

Phobias are regular and, to onlookers, unreasonable fears an individual may hold relating to specific circumstances or objects. For example, people suffering from agoraphobia may fear that they will panic and lose control of themselves in certain situations such as in supermarket queues or in other crowded places. Other common phobias can include fear of lifts, fear of spiders and fear of dental procedures.

A phobia is of serious concern when the symptoms are severe (for example, chest tightness, heart racing or pounding, shallow breathing, dizziness or trembling), or where it impacts significantly on your lifestyle (for example, not going on trips to the country just in case you happened to see a spider). The table below summarises the differences between anxiety, fear and phobia:

Anxiety A heightened sense that something bad may happen or of being on edge. Anxiety relates to a *non-specific, unrecognised danger*.

Fear Similar feelings to those experienced with anxiety except that the feelings relate to *recognisable, definable threats*. Examples include fear of possible attack if your car breaks down in a rough area of town at night, or the fear that a recent pathology test may return a positive result.

Phobia Phobias relate to specific places (for example, lifts), things (for example, spiders), or circumstances (for example, public speaking) that the person has learned to be afraid of but which are *generally unrealistic or unlikely to cause real harm*.

Depression

Most people suffer from some degree of depression at various times in their life. Depression may manifest itself as:

◆ feelings of hopelessness;

◆ inappropriate guilt;

◆ feelings of worthlessness;

◆ lack of energy;

◆ poor concentration;

◆ suicidal thoughts;

◆ social withdrawal; or

◆ diminished enjoyment of, or interest in, life's normal activities.

When the symptoms of depression are severe, prolonged or impinge on one's quality of life, it is important to seek professional assistance.

The causes of depression are complex and not easy to explain in a few words. However, in very basic terms there are two sources of depression:

◆ The natural response to events such as retrenchment, significant life changes such as retirement, divorce or the death of a close friend or relative. This type of depression is sometimes called *reactive depression* because it results from our reaction to an event or an aspect of our lifestyle.

◆ Depression that comes from the internal chemistry of the brain or from some other organic source. Where such depression has a genetic basis it is called *endogenous depression*.

Stress/burnout/post-traumatic stress

Psychologically based stress involves feelings of depression and anxiety resulting from one's *perceived inability* to cope with a particular set of circumstances. The words 'perceived inability' are particularly important, because what is stressful to one person may not be to another. For example, while some people may find the prospect of running a large multinational organisation stressful, the current Chief Executive may thrive in the role. Similarly, while performing an appendectomy is a routine task for many surgeons, it would be highly stressful for someone without medical training who was forced to operate in an emergency.

'I need to exercise my mind—I think stress is good in my case!'

This person was actually referring to a phenomenon known as 'facilitating anxiety', that is, the level of pressure needed to motivate yourself to action. However, the sentiments of what he said are true! Where high performing individuals are used to working under pressure, they will often report that they find the sudden absence of work pressure 'stressful'.

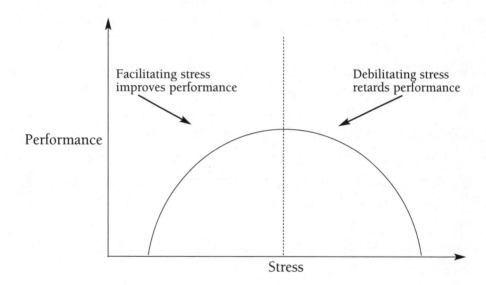

Stress may also be caused by physical conditions such as extreme temperature, high caffeine intake, infection, overexercising or exposure to some chemicals including alcohol and drugs. Where both psychological *and* physiological stress are present, the cumulative effects of both can be significant. For example, consider the difference between having to change a tyre on your car when you are running late for an appointment (psychological stress) versus having an entire afternoon to get the job done. If it was also a day when the temperature was over 35° Celsius (physiological stress), you can picture how the two stressors would combine to make the net effect greater than the sum of each stressor.

Stress can also occur in the form of burnout, where one becomes overwhelmed from prolonged exposure to a demanding role, such as working in a high pressure job or caring for a terminally ill loved one.

> *'I sometimes feel like climbing to the top of a mountain and staying there for about a year. When I eventually came down again, I would start saying "no" to many of those people who keep asking for my services.'*

This participant in the *Retire 200* project described his reaction to stress in a rather poetic way. His problem started when, soon after retirement, he agreed to join the committee of a voluntary organisation. His past business experience and natural tendency to get things done resulted in the committee being highly successful and he was soon invited to join other committees. Eventually he found that he had little time to himself and was actually experiencing a form of activity-related stress at a time when he wished to have a more relaxed lifestyle.

Most people have heard of the term 'post-traumatic stress'. This specific type of stress results from exposure to the overwhelming effects of a situation, such as arriving home to find your house burned to the ground, or losing all your savings in a recession. The causes of post-traumatic stress, relate to a highly significant or life-threatening event that has occurred where the sufferer feels they either have:

◆ little control over the circumstances,

◆ are not properly trained or prepared to deal with the event,

◆ or are under-resourced with equipment, funds or people.

During World Wars I and II post-traumatic stress was recognised under a number of labels ranging from 'war neurosis' to 'shell-shock'. Irrespective of the label, this type of post-traumatic stress was the understandable reaction of *normal* human beings who found themselves immersed in the horror of an *abnormal* situation.

Managing anxiety, depression and stress

NOTE: This section of the book is intended to help you develop strategies for managing emotional issues that may be impeding your ability to enjoy life. Consequently, the ideas provided should be seen in the context of 'self-development'. Where emotional problems such as anxiety or depression are seriously impacting on your lifestyle or have been present for a long time, or where thoughts of suicide are present, it is important that you seek professional advice from a suitably qualified practitioner.

The following text provides some ideas that have been helpful to others who have experienced anxiety and depression in their lives. Anxiety and depression are two quite different conditions and, because they have different symptoms and triggers, they are discussed separately.

Reducing the symptoms of anxiety

Relaxation, by definition, is the opposite of anxiety. It is therefore not surprising that many therapies for reducing anxiety focus on helping people to apply relaxation techniques. If you find that anxiety is affecting your life, then taking the time to apply relaxation techniques on a daily basis is highly recommended. Some ideas that you can immediately put into action include:

1. Breathing exercises using your diaphragm. The diaphragm is a set of muscles that helps the lungs inflate and deflate. If you look closely at someone who is sleeping you will see their diaphragm gently rising and falling as they breathe. On the other hand, an anxious person tends to take shallow, rapid breaths. By consciously using your diaphragm to breathe deeply and slowly you will find that your anxiety levels will gradually reduce. To do this:

- Lie down and put your hand on your abdomen (between your navel and your rib cage).

- Breathe in through your nose slowly and deeply. Your hand should rise as you breathe. Send the air far down to the bottom of your lungs. Try visualising what happens when you fill a bottle with water—the water enters the neck of the bottle and fills from the bottom up. Imagine that your lungs are the bottle and your nose is the opening of the bottle.

◆ Once you have filled your lungs, wait for a second or two and then breathe out fully through your nose or mouth. As you do this, let the muscles in your arms, legs and face relax so that your entire body is free from tension.

◆ Complete the above process ten times, remembering to do each round slowly. If you do this for five minutes, you will find that you feel more relaxed.

Note: If you start to feel a little light-headed during the breathing exercises, just stop for a minute or so then recommence.

2. Visualisation. When it comes to reducing anxiety, visualisation is a wonderful method of transporting yourself to a peaceful place where you can relax and recharge your batteries. For some, their ideal place may include the sounds of water rushing down a cool stream in the country, or it may be the sounds of the surf crashing onto the sands of a beach. For others, it could be a warm, comfortable room in a luxurious hotel on a snow-covered mountain.

The power of visualisation has long been recognised as a versatile and effective tool by psychologists. For example, athletes having a run of poor performance have been lifted back to their former levels simply by adding visualisation exercises to their training and preparation regime.

Consider this example of how I visualise my favourite place in the country where my wife and I go camping by the Acheron River in Buxton, Victoria.

It is early morning and I am lying under the warm doona in the tent. The cool, fresh air is gently blowing across my face through the tent window. Outside I can hear the sounds of birds marking their territories—the plaintive cry of ravens, the warbling of magpies and the distant laughter of kookaburras.

Nearby, the water is babbling over the small rocky ledge at the bend in the river as it winds its way down to the sea far away. The gurgling of the water, the gentle breeze rustling the leaves of the gum trees and the faint smell of the damp charcoal from last night's campfire merge to create the peace and tranquillity I love so much.

While I am immersed in the pleasures of this wonderful place I am breathing slowly and deeply—I feel relaxed, happy and peaceful.

Have a think about *your* ideal place, and then imagine yourself there taking it all in. If there is no actual place that you know of, invent one—it really does not matter. Write a description of what it is like and include not just the physical setting but the sounds you hear, the smells, what you are touching, how warm it is. Use as many of the five senses as possible when writing your description.

If you like, you can tape record yourself describing the scene so that you can lie back and play it when you are relaxing. You could also tape record the instructions for diaphragmatic breathing first so that your tape takes you on a relaxing journey, starting with the breathing exercises and ending at your favourite peaceful scene.

Reducing the symptoms of depression

'Life is boring. When I was alive I did things—now life is a living death with nothing to look forward to.'

When people are depressed they often experience what is known as the 'cognitive triad', that is, they have an unrealistically negative view of themselves, their environment and their future. The person quoted was clearly very depressed when we spoke. If you look at what she said, you will recognise the clear signs of the cognitive triad. If you are depressed and have been so for a long time it is wise to seek professional help. Depending on the type of depression you are experiencing, different types of therapy, including medication, may be required.

If you are presently suffering from depression and it is relatively short-lived, not causing you major problems such as suicidal thoughts and is related to a specific event such as adjusting to your lifestyle in retirement, then the following suggestions may be helpful.

1. Action: doing something is better than doing nothing. When someone is depressed, the prospect of taking simple actions such as telephoning a friend may be more then they can bear contemplating. It can be at times such as this that well-meaning friends or relatives may advise them to 'get out and do something' or to join a club and meet people. If you are presently depressed, you will know just how annoying and deflating such well-meaning advice can be.

On the other hand, evidence from clinical studies demonstrates that taking small steps such as getting out of the house and going up the street or walking through the park can help to relieve the symptoms of depression. It is certainly more uplifting than deciding to sit around and do nothing, even though this may seem preferable at the time.

2. Focus on what you are doing rather than on your depression. One of the reasons that action is more beneficial than inaction is that it provides you with the opportunity to take your mind off your depression, even if this is only for a short time. To maximise the benefit of any actions you make take, try to focus your attention on the details of what you are doing rather than on your depression. For example, if you are window shopping, focus on aspects of the products such as their colour, design etc. and begin to push your feelings of depression into the background.

3. Look at what has worked in the past. If your depression is relatively recent, you will be able to recall times when you took part in activities that you found interesting and enjoyable. Look back to those times when you were not depressed and make a list of the actions that you once found fun. You may find that as you develop your list, the activities do not seem to sound as enjoyable to you now as they once did. This is all part of the cognitive triad mentioned earlier. Notwithstanding this, set yourself the goal of undertaking one of these activities within a defined timeframe, for example, within one week. Take small steps at first and then, as you gain confidence, gradually increase your activities.

If your depression is due to the death of someone close and you find that your list of activities includes things you used to do with your deceased friend or partner, you may be saying, 'But it won't be as much fun now without _ _ _ _ _'. While this is probably true, it is still highly likely that involvement in the activity will be more beneficial than just staying home and doing nothing.

Reducing the symptoms of stress

The symptoms of stress are often close to those of anxiety. Consequently, many of the techniques that are used to successfully reduce anxiety can also help you to reduce your levels of stress.

If your stress results from a physical stressor such as substance abuse, you should seek professional advice regarding how to manage the problem. It is important to remember that in certain cases it is dangerous to go cold turkey by just ceasing to take a drug. The group of drugs known as benzodiazepines, which includes brand names such as Valium and Serapax, are examples of drugs that should only be withdrawn from under medical supervision.

In cases where stress is caused by exposure to a particular environment or lifestyle, then withdrawal from the situation is one solution. If this is not a practical option then relaxation exercises can help you through your stressful time.

Managing the causes of anxiety, depression and stress

The next section looks at a model used by psychologists when helping people deal with issues that impact on their well-being. The model is called Rational Emotive Therapy (RET) and is well established as a successful therapeutic process. RET is used successfully for treating problems ranging from simple phobias to serious cases of depression and anxiety.

Rational Emotive Therapy (RET)

Put simply, RET works on the basis that emotional problems such as anxiety and depression are often the by-product of the irrational or illogical beliefs that you have about yourself and the world around you. In other words, it is not *what* happens to you (for example, your car is stolen) that makes you angry, sad or depressed but rather what you say to yourself about what has happened ('This is terrible—I cannot stand it'). Where your belief system and self-talk is irrational or illogical then your emotional reactions to events will also be dysfunctional ('Because I cannot stand it, I am depressed').

When people are being introduced to RET for the first time they sometimes find the term 'irrational' offensive. However, it is important to remember that in the context of RET, 'irrational' does not imply mental illness. Rather, it describes the tendency to let your feelings and behaviours be ruled by the untested, unproven beliefs that you have and which can cause you unnecessary anxiety or depression.

The goal of RET is to therefore show people how to re-examine their thoughts, belief systems and self-talk so that they can then challenge and dispute the validity of any irrational or illogical beliefs that they discover. The next step is to replace these irrational beliefs with rational alternatives.

RET practitioners refer to the 'ABCs' of RET:

(A) There is an 'Activating' event, that is, the thing that happens to you, for example, 'I lost the part-time job I found soon after I retired.'

(B) Your 'Belief system' interprets the event, for example, 'This is terrible, without this job I am a worthless person.'

(C) You experience the emotional 'Consequences' of your interpretation, for example, 'Because I believe this is "terrible" and because I believe that I am a "worthless" person I now become depressed, anxious and sad.'

Consider the following example of how untested, irrational beliefs can impact on your well-being. Imagine that John has just come home from his club and is reflecting on an experience he had there today.

A = Activating event		B = Belief system		C = Consequences
'Today I was snubbed by Colin, the club president and the most popular member of the club.'	+	'Because Colin likes most members of the club, I am obviously *terribly boring*. This situation is *awful* and *I can't stand it*. Clearly, I am a *worthless* person and *must* resign from the club.'	=	'I feel *bitter, angry, rejected* and *depressed*.'

You can probably already see the flaws or irrational beliefs that are causing John's distress. Apart from the fact that Colin's 'snub' may have been unintentional, there are real flaws in the logic of John's belief system.

Try it again after John has challenged the validity of his irrational beliefs and replaced them with rational alternatives.

A = Activating event		B = Belief system		C = Consequences
'Today Colin, the most popular member of the club, failed to acknowledge me when I greeted him.'	+	'Either Colin did not hear me, or, he is in a bad mood, or he simply does not like me. If Colin does not like me this is *unfortunate* because I like him. However, the fact that he may not like me does not mean that I am worthless, unlikeable or a failure.'	=	'I feel *disappointed* and would *prefer* that Colin liked me. I am *saddened* and *a little annoyed* by this possibility but not depressed.'

You can see from the above example that John's response is more logical and stands up to scrutiny. Instead of a 'terrible' situation that he 'can't stand' and which renders him a 'worthless' person, the more rational John regards the situation realistically as 'unfortunate'. Instead of feeling 'bitter, angry, rejected and depressed', John is 'disappointed' and would 'prefer' that he was accepted. Consequently he is now 'saddened' and 'annoyed' rather than 'depressed'.

At this stage you may be saying to yourself, 'Surely just changing the way we describe an event to ourselves can't make all that much difference.' However, the fact remains that there have been countless experiments around the world that continue to validate the premise that where individuals modify their irrational belief systems and self-talk, they also change their emotions and behaviours.

The ten most common irrational beliefs

Most cognitive psychologists agree that everyone has a number of irrational beliefs that they need to regularly challenge and modify if they are to lead happy, fulfilling lives. Albert Ellis, the founder of Rational Emotive Therapy, argued that there are ten commonly recurring irrational beliefs that he encountered during his many years of psychological practice.

Irrational belief number one: 'I must have the love and approval of all the people I find significant.'
Rational alternative: Everyone *desires* and *wants* the approval of others and would be *less happy* without it. However, we do not *need* the approval of others. Saying that you *need* it implies that you would literally shrivel up and die without it.

Irrational belief number two: 'I must be competent or talented in some significant area of life.'
Rational alternative: While it would be *pleasant* to be talented and competent at something, it is not critically important. The problem with irrational belief number two is that it is often associated with the belief that you *are* what you do, for example, you *are* a doctor. In fact, nobody *is* a doctor. Some people work *as* a doctor, but they may also be working *as* a parent and *as* a grower of prize roses.

Irrational belief number three: 'When people act unfairly or nastily, they are bad people who should be punished.'

Rational alternative: Ask yourself, 'Where is it written that so-and-so *shouldn't* behave in this manner to you? Where is the proof that they *mustn't* act this way?' It would be *preferable* that they didn't act as they do, but hardly *essential*.

Irrational belief number four: 'When things do not go the way I would like them to it is awful, horrible and terrible and I can't stand it.'

Rational alternative: Although it may be *unfortunate* or *unpleasant* when things do not work out the way you would like them to, you *can* stand it. It may be less than what you want, and consequently regretful, but you *can* stand it.

Irrational belief number five: 'Emotional misery and distress come from external sources and I have no ability to control or change my feelings.'

Rational alternative: Much of the pain other people or events allegedly 'cause' results from taking rejection or criticism too seriously. You tell yourself that you *cannot stand it* when some people do not approve of you, and that life is *totally worthless* without their approval. However, if you examine this thinking further it is clear you will not cease to exist if your next door neighbours suddenly indicate that they prefer the company of others. You can therefore modify your thinking to something like: 'I would *greatly prefer* that my neighbours liked me and would feel *much more comfortable* with this situation. However, if they are determined to dislike me, *I can stand it* although *I don't like it*.'

Irrational belief number six: 'If something seems dangerous or to be feared I must be preoccupied with it, dwell on it possibly occurring and become anxious about it.'

Rational alternative: If something is dangerous then you can take action to avoid it where possible. If there is nothing you can do about it, you can stop yourself from the self-defeating practice of exaggerating its effects and making yourself miserable. For example, if you live near the rainforests of Queensland, there will be deadly taipan snakes in the area. However, constantly dwelling on the possibility of being bitten would be unhelpful.

Irrational belief number seven: 'It is easier to avoid many of life's difficulties and responsibilities than to apply self-discipline.'

Rational alternative: When you avoid your responsibilities, you are usually exaggerating the level of difficulty and discomfort they involve. You may also be afraid of trying in case you fail. However, failing is a natural part of the continual learning process everyone experiences. It can be helpful to remember that most experts in a particular skill have only become proficient by repeatedly doing it poorly and failing many times.

Irrational belief number eight: 'My past is all-important—because something once strongly influenced my life, it will go on determining my feelings and behaviour now.'

Rational alternative: By allowing yourself to blame past experiences for today's feelings and behaviours, you are actually taking the easy way out by not seeking new solutions to your problems. If you continue to act in a certain way, just because you have done so in the past, you deny yourself new experiences that may bring new rewards and solutions.

Irrational belief number nine: 'People and things should turn out better than they are—it is awful and horrible when you do not find solutions to life's hard realities.'

Rational alternative: There is no compelling reason why anyone or anything *should* be better just because you want this to be the case. While it would be *preferable* if things were better, you are just displaying a childishly low tolerance for frustration when you say, 'Things *should* be better and *I can't stand it* when they are not!'

Irrational belief number ten: 'I can obtain maximum happiness in life by doing as little as possible and by concentrating on enjoying myself to the full.'

Rational alternative: Most people find that they need to be doing something active and to be goal-oriented. Sitting around doing nothing may be fine when you are on a holiday, however, doing nothing all the time rarely suits intelligent people.

How many of the top ten irrational beliefs were among yours?

Applying RET to your life

First, identify the situations that you find cause you to feel anxious or upset. Make a list of them on the left-hand side of a sheet of paper. Such events may include those of the type described in the top ten above, or may relate to your own specific issues.

Second, try to identify what upsets you about the event. What are you saying to yourself about the event? Do you hear extreme terms like 'must never', or 'I can't stand it' or 'they should always . . .'? Write your self-talk down on the right-hand side of the paper next to the situations that cause you anxiety or depression. Where you detect unprovable, illogical self-talk then you will need to modify it to a more logical alternative.

Third, once you believe you have modified your irrational beliefs and self-talk to more rational alternatives, try imagining the event that was causing you distress. Listen to your new, modified self-talk and estimate the effect the event now has on you. Do you feel better about the event? If not, you may need to revisit your beliefs and self-talk again.

Some readers may be asking themselves right now, 'But if my self-talk is so faulty or illogical, how will I know?' This is a good question! For RET and indeed most psychotherapies to work effectively it is advisable to use a professional counsellor such as a psychologist to help you challenge your irrational self-talk. Just leaving this task to yourself encourages your natural tendency to deny the existence or magnitude of personal problems.

One idea that can help increase the likelihood of RET working without the presence of a psychologist is to first think of three compassionate, intelligent people that you greatly respect. They may still be living, or they may be people from the past such as a long dead but highly respected teacher or relative. Work through the three steps for applying RET listed above but use your imaginary 'panel' of wise and caring people to assess your self-talk. What do you think their reactions would be to your self-talk?

Another way to test the logic of your self-talk is to say it out aloud to yourself. Does your self-talk sound as logical when spoken aloud as it did when you were just thinking it?

Write down your self-talk and contrast it with rational alternatives. Consider the following example.

Irrational	Rational
(what you are saying to yourself now)	(your written rational alternative)
'I *always* get nervous when asked to speak at my club meeting. *I can't stand it* and I know I will *never* be any good at it.'	'So far, I have found that public speaking makes me *very nervous*. However, there is no reason why this should continue if I seek help, for example, by joining a public speaking group such as Rostrum.'

Where you find that certain events or situations upset you, draw a four-cell table like the one above and write down your present self-talk with a rational alternative. This process will help you modify your irrational self-talk.

More examples of using RET to change irrational beliefs or self-talk

Irrational	Rational
'It would be awful/terrible if I did not get elected president of the club.'	'It would be very disappointing if I did not get the presidency but it would hardly be the end of the world.'
'I am no good at arithmetic and I'll never be able to work out my tax return.'	'So far, I have not performed well at arithmetic, but that does not mean that with some help I cannot improve in the future.'

Irrational	**Rational**
'I am a hopeless failure at social functions.'	'I have sometimes performed poorly at social functions but with some work and advice I will be able to improve.'
'Living on the pension is killing me— I must have a high standard of living because when I don't, I can't stand it.'	'I would very much like to have a higher standard of living and I get annoyed that I don't. However, I can stand it and can adjust to it.'

These examples show that much of our faulty thinking and belief systems results from our tendency to:

Catastrophise situations, for example, 'I was twenty minutes late for my luncheon appointment with Sue today and she was clearly very annoyed. I will probably lose her friendship now and eventually will have no friends left at all.'

Fall victim to I-can't-stand-it, for example, 'When people are rude to me I can't stand it and believe that they should be punished.'

Allow extreme words such as *never* and *can't*, as well as directives such as *shouldn't*, *couldn't* and *mustn't*, become part of your thinking and self-talk, for example, 'I'll never be able to get up and address the members of the club — I always get nervous and I can't stand it when people see me like that!'

CHECKLIST

❑ I now understand the differences between anxiety, depression and stress.

❑ I know how to apply diaphragmatic breathing to reduce anxiety and stress.

❑ I know how to use visualisation to reduce anxiety and stress.

❑ I understand the importance of taking small active steps to reduce depression.

❑ I understand how Rational Emotive Therapy can help reduce feelings of depression, anxiety and stress.

❑ I have used RET to work on one area of my life that causes me to become anxious, stressed or depressed.

Chapter 11

Building and maintaining self-esteem

The aims of this chapter are to:

◆ examine the relationship between how you see yourself (your self-concept) and how you regard yourself (self-esteem);

◆ identify the causes and effects of low self-esteem on your life; and

◆ examine ways of building self-esteem to increase your enjoyment of life.

What is self-esteem?

Self-esteem can be described as the sum of your levels of self-respect and self-acceptance. Self-esteem affects the way you behave, think and feel. When you are suffering from low self-esteem you may find that you are depressed, anxious and lack self-confidence. Consequently, you may go through life short-changing yourself by denying your natural abilities and your right to realise your full potential.

Conversely, when you have healthy levels of self-esteem you also have healthy levels of self-respect. You open yourself to more of life's options because you correctly believe that you deserve them.

Self-esteem behaviours

Some of the behaviours that may be found in people who have low levels of self-esteem include:

They may have trouble saying no. Lack of belief in themselves leads people with low self-esteem to want to please others as a way of gaining acceptance.

They may find it difficult to accept a compliment graciously. Because their self-esteem is low, they do not believe they are worthy of the compliments they may receive.

They may take little care with their appearance and grooming. They may believe that attending to grooming will make little difference because they know they are unlikeable or unattractive anyway. Lack of care with grooming may also be a by-product of the depression that can accompany low self-esteem.

They fear rejection from their peers and others. Because their belief in themselves is already fragile, they believe that others will reject them and therefore they withdraw from social interaction before this can occur.

They find it difficult to list their positive points. Because their self-concept is low, they may not believe that they have positive aspects to their personality or appearance.

They may make regular self-disparaging comments about themselves, their abilities, their appearance. In some cases this may be a strategy to stop others from getting in first with hurtful criticisms. In other cases, it is done in the hope that others will disconfirm their criticism and bolster their self-esteem by saying something like, 'No! You're not really fat!'

Self-concept

Your level of self-esteem is dependent on your self-concept, that is, the way in which you perceive yourself. Self-concept is sometimes broken down into seven sub-sets:

1. Intellectual self-concept. The way you rate yourself as you compare your thinking ability or your intelligence to that of your peers and others around you.

2. Personal self-concept. How you evaluate your personality and your sense of adequacy when you compare yourself to others around you.

3. Social self-concept. How you perceive your skills at social interaction compared to other people with whom you socialise.

4. Family self-concept. Your perception of yourself when you examine your worth or contribution as a family member.

5. Physical self-concept. How you perceive your physical condition compared to others—the way you look, your own state of health…

6. Moral self-concept. How you rate yourself based on your personal ethics or moral code. For some people this also includes their relationship with their religion and their consequent self-rating as a 'good' or 'bad' individual.

7. Behavioural-action self-concept. How you rate yourself based on your behaviours and activities, for example, your perceptions of yourself as lazy versus diligent, constructive versus destructive…

Interestingly, aspects of self-concept adversely affecting one person can impact quite differently on the self-esteem of another person. For example, an obese teenage girl may be distressed about her body shape because the messages she receives daily from the media, her peers and members of her family continually reinforce the idea that being fat is not 'cool.' On the other hand, an overweight opera singer may not care less about his obesity. His high levels of self-esteem may be dependent on his ability to use his talent and on the adulation he receives from his audience. Similarly, a Japanese sumo wrestler may actually regard his obesity positively due to its high levels of acceptance among his peers and fans.

The good news for everyone is that self-esteem influenced by aspects of your negative self-concept can be counter-balanced by self-esteem based on positive aspects of your self-concept. Consequently, if someone is overweight they can learn to enjoy a high level of self-esteem by focusing on their intellectual or artistic abilities.

How self-concept is formed

Much of your self-concept is shaped by the influences of the adults in your life when your personality was developing. At this time, when you were dependent on adults such as your parents, grandparents and teachers, your self-worth or self-concept was influenced by the quality and consistency of the positive feedback they provided. If you were lucky and were surrounded by nurturing adults, you had a good chance of emerging from childhood with a well-rounded, healthy self-concept.

Listed here are seven broad areas where childhood exposure to adults impacts on the formation of self-concept:

Highly critical or demanding parents/teachers. Naturally, parents should encourage their children to perform at their best and to take pride in their achievements. However, if parents set standards for their children that are too high, their children are destined to fail repeatedly. For example, some parents put undue pressure on their child to come first in the class or to excel at sport. In many instances, these parents are attempting to relive their own lives through their children and in doing so unwittingly impose immense psychological pressure on them. Such experiences can leave children feeling defeated and guilty as they struggle to succeed where the odds are stacked against them. Moreover, because children usually have no way of knowing that the demands being placed on them are unreasonable, they naturally assume that they are at fault when they do not live up to their parents' expectations.

Children of famous or very successful parents. Children of highly successful parents can also fall victim to low self-concept. Where a parent is an outstanding success, particularly in a highly visible setting such as business, sport or the arts, it is very difficult for the child to compare their own endeavours favourably. The problem can be compounded if the parent is frequently absent due to the demands their success makes on them—this further deprives the child of the consistent positive reinforcement and nurturing they require.

Exposure to strict codes of behaviour. Negative influences on a child's self-concept can occur in an environment that prescribes certain behaviours as good, and proscribes others as bad or 'sinful'. A common feature of these settings occurs when the child's successes are regarded as a 'gift from God' for which the child should be 'thankful'. However, when the child fails it is attributed to their laziness or to some other personal deficit. In such an environment the child is in a no-win situation, denied positive self-esteem for their successes, but blamed for their failures.

Abusive parents/teachers. Children who have been physically or sexually abused by adults often find that they have an array of confused feelings including guilt, personal inadequacy, rage, insecurity and the inability to trust others. Where trust is diminished people risk becoming emotionally isolated, which leads to poor self-concept and attending low self-esteem.

At the heart of child abuse is the shattering of children's natural preparedness to trust in the safety of adults. Tragically, those who prey on children often manoeuvre themselves into positions of trust or authority where the child may actually be encouraged by their parents to place their trust with the very person abusing them.

Abandonment. A healthy self-concept is established within an environment of care and positive reinforcement. However, if children feel abandoned by their parents they may regard themselves as not important enough to be loved. Abandonment can take a number of forms. Sometimes it involves literal separation; on other occasions, it is a case of psychological abandonment. Consider the following examples:

◆ The parent rejects the child. Rejection may take the form of being fostered or adopted out of the family, or it may be rejection in the form of coldness or indifference on the part of one or both of the parents. In some cases, the parent may be attempting to manage personal problems such as depression or physical illness. In these cases it may simply be beyond their emotional resources to attend to their child while dealing with their own illness and the concurrent financial problems that often are a by-product of such situations.

◆ There can also be cases of 'psychological' abandonment. For example, where the mother and father are very young themselves they may find the unrelenting demands of child-rearing too much to handle. This problem is compounded where a single parent is raising the child alone and is required to subsist on a single parent's pension.

◆ The effect of divorce on children has been the subject of numerous studies on the comparative benefits to the child of staying in a disruptive, unhappy home compared with living with one parent and seeing the other periodically. In either case, the child is often on the perimeter of their parents' disputes and acrimony, and may form the opinion that *they* are in some way to blame for their parents' distress.

◆ Finally, there is the sense of abandonment in childhood that accompanies the death of a parent. Where the child is very young they may have difficulty understanding why a parent has left them to 'go to heaven' and may feel that they have been abandoned. The sense of abandonment can then be compounded by changes in the household environment as the surviving parent attempts to raise the child while managing their own grief under difficult circumstances.

Parents with addictions. Without a reliable and consistent environment children become confused and insecure. Where parents are addicted to alcohol or drugs they are rarely able to provide a stable environment. Consequently, behaviour of the child's that is applauded and encouraged one day when everyone is drunk or high may be condemned and result in corporal punishment the next time the parents are hung-over or withdrawing. Naturally, this unpredictable environment causes children to lose confidence in their own judgment.

Where hard drugs are involved, the parents invariably associate with other addicts who may be the only other people who understand and tolerate their behaviour. Consequently, the child receives mixed messages as they grapple to adjust to chaos and instability at home on one hand, and the structured, predictable life they experience at school.

At a psychological level the child sees their addicted parent(s) denying the problem of their addiction and may also learn that denying their own feelings is the best strategy to use to deal with their own pain and confusion.

Overindulgent parents. Most of us can remember childhood peers who were 'spoiled rotten'. It seemed that they were the luckiest kids we knew—they always got what they wanted for birthdays and Christmas and always seemed to have the latest toys or clothes. The problem for such children, however, is that they may never learn to postpone pleasant events. Consequently, in adulthood they can find life immensely frustrating if they cannot get what they want NOW! Adulthood can be a continual disappointment if life fails to deliver the rewards that appeared on a platter in childhood. The major risks associated with such conditioning are boredom with the drabness of life, or financial disasters caused by the inability to defer purchasing desired goods on credit or to manage money appropriately.

Self-esteem and retirement

The changes to your lifestyle that follow retirement can impact both positively and negatively on your self-esteem. Many of the participants in the *Retire 200* program were relieved to hear that they were not alone when it came to being negatively affected by retirement. In particular, some people felt embarrassed about admitting that they missed the status of their job.

> 'Over the years I have got into the habit of asking people that I am being introduced to about what line of work they are in. It has always been a good ice-breaker for me, especially since I was proud of my own occupation as manager of an engineering section of BHP. Soon after retirement, I found that I felt awkward when meeting people because I had lost my old patter. It really knocked my self confidence around for a while.'

The research identified eleven aspects of retirement that impacted on self-esteem. These are looked at briefly here and are followed by ways in which to boost your self-esteem if any of them are issues for you.

Loss of identity

'It is so easy to describe yourself as "unimportant' because you are not working or earning money.'

'You must view yourself as "somebody".'

Some people describe themselves as being devalued by not having a role to play in the workforce. Psychologists frequently encounter this problem, not just with those in retirement, but with those who have lost their jobs due to organisational closure, retrenchment or ill-health. From a psychological point of view the person may be identifying with the job. For example, instead of saying, 'I work *as* an engineer' a person may say, 'I *am* an engineer.' Where such faulty logic is used, the corollary is that in retirement, 'I am a nothing!'

Loss of status

Where a retired person's former role comprised a high status occupation such as the Chief Executive Officer or the National Sales Manager they not only lose their career, but also the status provided by their organisational title and its benefits.

Loss of purpose

For many people, going to work each day provides them with a purpose in life, such as making a worthwhile contribution at work, interacting with colleagues or contributing to the financial welfare of their family. When these people retire they may find a number of areas of their self-concept are affected, for example, their social self-concept, family self-concept and personal self-concept.

Loss of structure

People who have found security from working in highly structured work environments may suffer a loss of self-esteem if they find themselves locked into a comparatively aimless lifestyle soon after retiring. There are a number of ways of establishing structure in retirement. The simplest and most widely used is maintaining a diary or wall planner that you fill with events and appointments. These events can range from having lunch with a friend to attending club meetings or the annual general meetings of organisations in which you have shares.

Social stereotypes

The impact of social stereotypes can impinge on the self-esteem of those who have retired, especially those who do so at a comparatively young age. The work ethic in Australia is such that society often questions the moral strength of those who are not gainfully employed. In many cases, such judgmental attitudes are inappropriate yet still affect people who may have no logical reason to feel guilty. The work ethic is so entrenched in some people that even when they are retired they still feel guilty if they are not doing something constructive. One man could not bring himself to turn on the television set during the day because this represented idleness to him. Others felt inappropriately guilty accepting the age pension because they viewed it as a hand-out rather than a benefit that had been funded from their years of paying income tax.

Reduction in income

Very few people are able to generate the same levels of income that they enjoyed during their working life. Consequently, lifestyle adjustments usually need to be made if financial resources are to last. People who had planned for their retirement and who had agreed together on how to adjust their spending patterns before retirement were usually much better off emotionally than those who had not planned. The latter tended to wake up to the realisation that they were going to need to reduce spending far more than they had anticipated. For example, the former practice of going to a restaurant once a week may now not be possible. Self-esteem can take a battering under these circumstances, particularly if dining out has been with a group of friends who can still afford it.

Loss of important social networks

In every organisation there are people who are prepared to dedicate much of their spare time to organising social events for staff. These events may range from raffles and other fund-raising ideas for charities to playing the role of Father Christmas at the office party. Notwithstanding the pay-off to the organisation from increased morale and team building, these natural organisers thoroughly enjoy their roles. Consequently, on retiring it is important that such people quickly capitalise on their skills as organisers by establishing themselves as active members of clubs or voluntary organisations.

Changed relationships

The relationship between partners is usually affected when one or both retire. Roles such as doing the shopping or mowing the lawn may have been designated on the basis that the balance between the rigours of a career and home maintenance needed to be fairly distributed. (The arguments reported by *Retire 200* participants over what constituted a 'fair' distribution of duties would fill a book on its own!) However, when both partners are retired and at home all day the lines between who should do what can blur.

Lack of activity

The need for purposeful activities is addressed in detail in Chapter 1. However, it is clear that when retired people are not involved in sufficient hours of such activity each week, they are at risk from anxiety, depression and stress, any one of which can impact on their levels of self-esteem.

Substance abuse

In many cases, substance abuse is simply the by-product of boredom or loneliness. Seeking refuge in alcohol or drugs can be a significant risk factor where people are living alone. Former drinking habits may gradually change from enjoying one or two glasses of wine with dinner to commencing drinking earlier in the day. As alcohol is a depressant, such drinkers may find that lethargy and alcohol-related illnesses can lead to the abuse of painkillers. One of the first casualties of such addiction is self-esteem.

Destructive pastimes

Several retired people raised the issue of destructive pastimes such as problem gambling. Like substance abuse, gambling problems often started because of boredom or loneliness. Gambling includes betting, where bets are placed on a race; gaming, where money is wagered on the result of a game such as cards or roulette; and lotteries, where money purchases numbers to be drawn from a pool.

The proliferation of gambling outlets dispersed conveniently around the suburbs has made those with a gambling problem or suffering from boredom a likely target. In recent times the gaming industry has identified women as a growth market and it is now strategically designing their venues to provide a safe and entertaining environment.

Self-esteem is affected by gambling in a number of ways. However, two significant areas that were raised by the research were:

◆ The impacts on financial health where the main earning years are over. Guilt and despair follow as losses are chased and more money is diverted from retirement savings.

◆ The compulsive nature of gambling causes reductions in self-esteem where gamblers view themselves as being locked into a habit that is beyond their control.

Ways to improve self-esteem

Challenge the voices from the past

If you think back to your childhood you may be able to recall the types of criticisms you received from teachers, parents and your peers. Down one side of a piece of paper list the negative or hurtful comments that you recall people making and which still bother you. Counter them with your own comments on the other side. Some examples of how to reject the voices from the past are shown in the following table. Develop your own list and read it when you are feeling down.

'You are lazy...'	'I am not lazy. I work long and hard in certain areas of my life. However, I do have quite different priorities in life to [Mary, John] which may be giving them the impression that I am lazy.'
'You are dumb...'	'I may not live up to [Sue's, Peter's] expectations in some ways. However, intelligence and common sense take a number of forms. I believe I have made many intelligent decisions in my life.'
'You are vain...'	'I take pride in my appearance because I enjoy looking good and feeling good about myself. I also believe that grooming is important [in business and to set an example for my children]. If some people interpret the way I attend to my grooming as "vanity" I cannot be concerned about their views.'
'You are a failure...'	'It is true that a number of aspects of my life have not turned out as well as I would have liked them to. However, there is a big difference between failing and being a "failure". Furthermore, part of the reason I sometimes fail is my preparedness to try new ideas. If people don't try anything new they can't fail at it! However, I would rather keep on trying even if it means I continue to fail from time to time.'

Building self-esteem through group membership

'You need emotional support if you are unmarried and do not have close family—for me it is belonging to my church.'

Some people gain comfort and social support from belonging to a religious group and describe a deep sense of spiritual belonging and comfort from their religious beliefs. Others, however, were less religious but valued membership of a church because of the social life and the network of caring people who were there for each other in times of need.

The shoebox method

Some years ago a convention relating to self-esteem and motivation was organised. One of the platform speakers was an insurance salesman who, after many years in the industry, had risen to the top of the sales ladder. It had been no easy feat. As we listened, he described the rejection he experienced ten to twenty times a day as he approached prospective clients hoping to discuss their insurance needs. Can you imagine what it would be like to be rejected, often rudely, day in and day out, year after year?

During the speech, this hardened sales veteran held up a battered shoebox and described to the audience the role it played in his ability to remain motivated in such a harsh psychological environment. In the shoebox were scraps of paper on which were written the details of achievements and events of which he was proud. Included in the box was a letter of thanks from the widow of a former client whose insurance policy had paid out a mortgage. There were also notes of thanks for the talks he had given to clubs and schools, and a birthday card made for him by his five-year-old grand-daughter.

Every time this salesman felt depressed, he would sit down with the shoebox and read the contents to energise himself. As new, positive experiences occurred in his life he would write them down on scraps of paper and add them to the box. He claimed that the process of reading the contents of his shoebox never failed to rejuvenate him. Many of my clients now successfully use the shoebox technique during times when they are feeling down.

List your good points

The shoebox method demonstrates how you can keep a record of communications from others who have recognised your achievements. For some, however, this may be a difficult task. You may simply not move in circles where you are likely to attract the sort of public attention that results in testimonials. You may also be a quiet achiever who simply does not draw attention to yourself, or you may possess the types of qualities that do not attract letters, cards and acclaim. If this is true there is still much you can do without the input of others. Try asking yourself the following questions, then supply your own responses.

Some questions you can use	Your answers
'Am I a good friend to anyone?'	
'Am I loyal?'	
'Who are the people who like me?' (If some of these people are now deceased still include them)	
'Am I punctual?'	
'Am I well organised?'	
'What do I do well at home?'	
'What do I do well when I am with my friends?'	
'What was something my best friend at school liked about me?'	
'What do my children, grandchildren and friends like about me?'	
'What do I like about my looks?'	
'How have I ever managed my way through a difficult time in the past?'	
'Do I have a good sense of humour?'	
'Do I try new things from time to time?'	
'Do I have a nice laugh?'	

Try adding your own questions (especially if you think you may have a good answer).

When you have generated your list and can think of no more questions, turn the ones with positive answers around and make them statements. For example, if the answer to 'Am I loyal?' is 'Yes', then write down 'I am loyal because I ...'. Continue to write down statements for all the questions with positive answers and make up your own shoebox to put them in. As you think of other good aspects of your personality, appearance or behaviours add them to the shoebox. Make sure you keep them handy to read when you are feeling down.

Twelve ideas for building self-esteem

Listed here are twelve ideas you can apply to build your levels of self-esteem.

Accept yourself for who you are. We all have strengths and weaknesses. Before we can improve our areas of weakness we need to accept ourselves as fallible human beings. Then, once we start to feel okay about ourselves we will find that we are more likely to take risks and to 'have a go' at change.

Forgive yourself. We have all said and done things in the past that we regret. However, the 'past has passed'. Instead of dwelling on how it could have been, regard your mistakes as opportunities to learn and grow. If there are areas of your past life that continue to cause you regret or distress, do something positive or helpful for someone *now* to balance the wrong you believe you are responsible for in the past.

Understand and forgive the imperfections of others. When the origins of self-concept were discussed earlier in this chapter, you may have found yourself getting angry as you recalled aspects of your own childhood. Go back and think about the influences that may have caused those around you to be less than perfect. Think about the resources and help *they* may have lacked in their own lives and try to empathise with their situation. If you can't forgive them, at least try to understand that their actions were based on their own ignorance, lack of skill or personal deficits.

Don't just rely on external influences to feel good. If someone rejects you or behaves in a way that upsets you, focus your attention back on who you are. Remember your own good points and the positive things that you have achieved in your life such as making someone happy, listening to a friend who needed to talk or helping someone in distress.

Do something to be proud of. Add up your achievements like the salesman with the shoebox. Everyone has achieved something positive during their life. For example, once when I was working as a Lifeline telephone counsellor a young woman told me how she had walked to the local railway line with the intention of throwing herself under a train. She was suffering from severe depression associated with a psychiatric disorder, had no job, no friends and had been rejected by her family. On the way to the railway line she happened to pass a woman who smiled at her as their paths crossed. That simple act of pleasantness gave the young woman the strength to go on living for another day. So it is possible that we have all had a positive effect on others without even being aware of it.

Look after yourself. If you are over-tired or out of condition, you are more likely to become anxious and insecure, which in turn will impact negatively on your self-esteem. Try to get enough sleep, balance your diet and exercise regularly.

Accept your mistakes. Regard your mistakes as opportunities for growth. If you make a mistake do not try to pretend it has not happened or attempt to pass the blame on to others. Accept your mistakes and learn from them. Try to find ways to avoid similar mistakes in the future. Be prepared to say, 'I don't know' rather than bluffing your way through situations.

Set and attain some realistic goals. Achieving goals is one of the most satisfying accomplishments you can experience. Chapter 14 examines why some people are more naturally inclined to set goals than others. However, regardless of your natural tendency, you will find that setting goals and then achieving them does wonders for your self-esteem.

Goals can be long term and substantial such as completing a degree or renovating a house. You can also set short-term goals such as arriving at the decision to finally throw out all the junk you have been tripping over in your shed for the past year. If you have a history of starting projects that you rarely finish, plan your activity from start to finish. Make a list of the actions required to complete the task and tick them off as they are achieved.

Stop judging yourself harshly. Chapter 10 discussed how punishing yourself with the tyranny of the 'shoulds' and 'musts' can affect your emotional well-being. Part of accepting yourself includes replacing expressions such as 'I should do...' with 'I would like to do...' or 'It would be better if I did such and such ... but not essential.'

Mix with people who are positive. If you regularly associate with people who have a persistently negative attitude to life you will need extraordinary strengths to resist being dragged down by them. This does not mean that you should abandon friends or relatives who are experiencing personal problems. However, if you are the type of caring person who seems to attract troubled people in their droves, then make a conscious decision to limit the time you spend with them. You will be amazed at the effect of reducing time with negative people and replacing it with time with those for whom life is positive and exciting.

Replace negative self-talk with positive self-talk. Next time you are about to say or think something negative about someone—stop! Look for one of their better points. For example, replace, 'Jane is staid and boring' with 'Over the years Jane has proven herself to be a loyal and caring friend.' Of course, your replacement statement does need to be true!

Write a daily affirmation. At the end of each day, write down one point that makes you feel good about yourself. It could be a goal that you met, a kindness that you extended to another person or simply the completion of a particular project.

After you have made your daily list, keep it and add to it. This version of the shoebox will help you feel good about yourself when you find that your self-esteem is taking a battering.

CHECKLIST
- ❏ I understand the difference between 'self-concept' and 'self-esteem'.
- ❏ I have challenged destructive messages from the 'voices from the past'.
- ❏ I have started my own shoebox of positive feedback.
- ❏ I have studied the twelve ideas for building my self-esteem and have put a number of them into practice.

Chapter 12

Understanding grief and loss

The aims of this chapter are to:

- ◆ understand the effects of grief and loss;
- ◆ examine ways to help yourself during times of grief; and
- ◆ examine ways of helping others who are grieving.

Note: In this book there have been frequent references to the effect of retirement lifestyle issues on relationships. It is important to devote time to this because in retirement, people in relationships tend to spend much more time together. However, I have been conscious of the many people who will read this book who either do not have a partner or who have recently lost their partner due to death or separation. Where such frequent references to partners are a source of further pain to those living alone, I am truly sorry. I hope this chapter goes some way to helping you gain more of the happiness you deserve in retirement.

What is grief?

Grief consists of our physical, psychological and social responses to the loss of someone we love, or to whom we are closely bonded in friendship. While most people associate grief with the death of a person, the symptoms of grief may also arise due to the loss of our job on retirement, through the loss of a friendship or through divorce.

Because the range of emotions associated with grieving is so diverse and intense, those experiencing grief sometimes wonder if they are going crazy. Yet despite these feelings, grief is a very normal response to the tragedy of personal loss. In fact, psychologists who specialise in the area of grief counselling are far more likely to be concerned by a lack of demonstrable grief in a recently bereaved person than by the healthy process of grieving.

For how long do people grieve?

Over the years there have been a number of popular books published that describe the 'stages' of grief those in mourning experience. It has sometimes been easy to gain the impression from these books that grief is a predictable, orderly process whereby the mourner begins at one end, proceeds through a number of predictable stages, and emerges 'cured' at the other end. However, as people who have experienced it will tell you, the process of grieving rarely if ever has any bearing on logic. Each individual who experiences grief does so in their own way and in their own time.

While grief is very much an individual response to loss, there are usually a number of processes that those in mourning will share in common.

Shock

Where death has occurred suddenly, those who were close to the deceased will naturally experience shock. A sudden fatal heart attack or accidental death catapults loved ones into instant trauma. However, shock can still occur even when death is expected following a long illness, because those involved in caring for their loved one have typically been in a state of heightened anxiety and stress during the illness. Consequently, they have not had the time nor the emotional space to prepare themselves for their loved one's death.

To complicate matters further, there is often the desperate hope that a cure will be found or that the patient will live longer than the medical profession is predicting. These hopes and anxieties can create a high level of denial so that when death does eventually occur the shock is almost as severe as that experienced from a sudden death.

One symptom of the trauma in such circumstances is psychological or emotional 'numbness'. Many people describe how, immediately after the death of a loved one, their day-to-day life resembled a dream-like state in which they experienced feelings of being detached from reality. These feelings can go on for some days and it is common during these times to feel like a spectator looking on as the rest of the world goes by. Life may seem to consist of a series of actions occurring on automatic pilot where conscious decision-making is absent. Such emotional turmoil can be very frightening and sometimes sees people questioning their own sanity.

Denial

Denial can occur on a number of levels. The dying person and the loved ones will often remain in a state of denial regarding the terminal nature of the complaint. A typical response is 'This can't be happening to us!' or 'There must be some mistake—maybe the test results were for someone else.' In the case of divorce or separation, denial may take the form of 'Perhaps they will come back to me soon' or 'When they have got this temporary fling out of their system they will come running back.'

Remaining in denial has a number of negative side effects. The person who is dying may never have the opportunity to organise their affairs. Consequently, important matters such as making a will or arranging for power of attorney may be left until it is too late. This can cause financial and emotional difficulties for those surviving at the very time when they need as few worries as possible.

Where a person is in denial over a relationship that has ended, they continue to place themselves in a stressful no-man's land by putting off the day when they have to deal with their grief.

Psychological, physiological and social responses

Physical responses to grief include an increased vulnerability to stress-related illnesses, while psychological responses include anxiety and depression. At a social level, responses include the ways in which you find yourself interacting with your friends and family.

From the mourner's perspective, psychological and social responses to grief can be compounded by the observation that, while their own world seems to have ended, others around them soon return to their normal routines of work and family life. Looking on while friends and relatives appear to function unscathed by the loss often adds to the overwhelming sense of emptiness that many mourners feel.

Along with feelings of psychological isolation can come a range of other unwanted psychological effects. Some people describe feeling that they are becoming more like the deceased in a number of ways, and that aspects of the deceased's personality or repertoire of behaviours are being incorporated into their own personal make-up. At the same time, physical problems such as loss of appetite and sleep disturbances can emerge just as the grieving person is at their most vulnerable.

Guilt

Feelings of guilt invariably surface during the grieving process. Those close to the deceased may start to regret the way in which they had handled past disputes, or may regret that they had not done more for the deceased. They may also find themselves wishing that they had been more open about expressing love and affection for their loved one. Such guilt is usually misplaced and fails to take into account the personalities of the deceased and of those around them. For example, for some people hugging and public statements such as 'I love you' are difficult or embarrassing although they may seem like missed opportunities once the person has died.

Anger

Grieving relatives will often find themselves experiencing feelings of anger that, paradoxically, are directed towards the deceased: 'They had no right to leave me alone like this!' While this is a very common grieving response, it can also be a bewildering experience. However, it is normal during such times and, like many of the other responses to grief, does not mean that the person is going mad despite what they may be tempted to believe.

The person who is dying may also feel anger that they direct towards the medical profession for not having diagnosed the complaint earlier or treated the illness more successfully. As well, anger may result from the dying person's frustration that their long-term plans will not be completed.

The 'pedestal' effect

At some stage early in the grieving process people usually find themselves focusing on the good aspects of the deceased while ignoring, or even denying, their less pleasant sides. Sometimes when listening to grieving people reminisce it could be assumed that the deceased was a saint! However, after experiencing so much pain and shock, those left grieving are in desperate need of fond memories to reinforce the positive aspects of their relationship with the deceased.

Reality

During this stage, the bereaved will start to regain their view of the deceased person as a normal human being who had good and less favourable aspects to their make-up. It is during this time that the accuracy of statements such as, 'If only they were still alive I would never complain again!' are questioned as the bereaved puts a more realistic interpretation on their relationship with their late friend or partner.

Acceptance, adjustment and growth

These final grieving processes occur when the bereaved finally accepts their loss and acknowledges the need to move on as an individual. Where partnerships have been close knit, with most activities and social occasions carried out as a couple, the surviving partner may find that their first steps out into the world again are simultaneously daunting and exciting. It is during this time that fine tuning communication skills and the ability to manage anxiety become important (see Chapters 2 and 10).

Managing grief and loss

Support groups

Sometimes well-meaning people will say to a grieving friend or relative, 'I know how you feel.' They may then be surprised to hear the grieving person angrily snap back with 'How could you know how I feel?' In fact, the grieving person is correct! How could anyone else know how they feel if they have not experienced the circumstances the grieving person is going through? It is because of the need for people in mourning to share their grief with those who really understand that bereavement groups have formed. The thinking behind such self-help groups is that the only people who really know how others feel during grief are those who have experienced the same type of pain and loss.

Because each person grieves differently, self-help groups benefit some people more than others. People also differ regarding the timing of their attendance at self-help groups. For example, some people find themselves benefiting from self-help groups a couple of weeks after their partner's death. Others may wait months or years. Whatever the case, the important point to remember is that these self-help groups are designed to provide those who are grieving with a safe, supportive environment where they can share the burden of their pain and loneliness with others. The level of participation at self-help groups is voluntary, so that if an attendee just feels like sitting and listening while others discuss their own grief it is okay to do so.

There are many different types of self-help groups that have been formed to help people grieve about their particular type of loss. If you feel that you could benefit from attending a self-help group, contact your local library or community office for a list of the groups in your area.

Rebound relationships

'My husband and I had been close friends with the couple across the road for over thirty years—even our children went to the same school. When my husband died a year after my neighbour's wife we started going out just for

company. We married soon after because I thought I knew him so well. It wasn't until after our wedding that I discovered my mistake!'

Unfortunately, by the time people retire some have already lost their partner due to death. It is around our fifties and sixties that we begin to see an elevated incidence of death and terminal illness among our friends and family; in fact, a number of those participating in the *Retire 200* research retired early to care for an ill partner or family member. Sometimes these carers were eventually faced with the death of the person they were caring for and then found themselves dealing simultaneously with the joint issues of grief and adjustment to retirement.

During times such as these people are lonely and emotionally raw, and decisions to enter a new relationship may be made for the wrong reasons. The initial relief from loneliness may then only be short lived if the relationship is not founded on the important components of mutual trust and respect, commonality of interests and all of the other variables that make a relationship work.

Helping a grieving friend or relative

Because the death of someone close is such a traumatic experience, friends or relatives of the bereaved may desperately want to help but feel that they do not know what they should do. Usually this reluctance is either based on their own discomfort or the concern that if they do or say the wrong thing they will only make matters worse. However, what people really need when they are grieving is the company and support of those they are closest to. The very worst thing that people can do is to stay away from them when they need support most.

Of course, when you are helping people whose emotions are fragile it is wise to be prepared for their emotional responses to be quite different to the responses you have been used to during less stressful times. For example, a teenage boy visited the home of a friend whose father had died the previous day. Without thinking, he greeted his friend's mother with, 'How are things?' It was the type of automatic friendly greeting he usually gave her and he had clearly not thought through the type of reaction such a greeting could receive at this time. He was therefore horrified when she snapped back with an icy, 'Under the circumstances I think that is a most inappropriate question!' as she stormed out of the room.

Naturally everyone is different and will bring their own personality to the experience of grief. However, the following list of general do's and don'ts may help you if you are helping someone through the crisis of grief.

What to do

◆ If they wish to cry and to share their grief let them do so; do not try to stop them because *you* feel uncomfortable. It is a good emotional release for them and is part of a healthy grieving process.

◆ Tell them you are sorry for what has happened. Do not be afraid to say this in case you make them cry.

◆ Be available to listen to them and to help them with anything that seems to need doing.

◆ Encourage them to keep talking if they want to discuss their loved one.

◆ Encourage them to take sufficient time to get over the shock caused by the death of their friend or loved one. Many people will say things like, 'I should be getting over this by now', when in fact only a few weeks or months have passed.

What not to do

◆ Do not try to rush the grieving process by implying that the grieving person needs to put grief behind them as soon as possible.

◆ Do not tell them you 'know how they feel' unless you have been through a similar experience yourself. Even where you have suffered a similar loss, the grieving person may feel that their own grief is more severe due to the special relationship they felt they had with their friend or partner.

◆ Do not avoid those in mourning because you feel you do not have anything to offer them. Your company and concern will be invaluable to them. If they genuinely wish to be left alone at times, you should of course respect that too.

◆ Do not try to change the subject when they want to discuss their loved one. People will sometimes do this in the genuine belief that they are saving the grieving person from unnecessarily upsetting themselves. However, the process of talking about their loved one is important at this time.

◆ Do not avoid using the deceased's name for fear of upsetting the person in mourning.

◆ Do not attempt to look for positive aspects of the deceased's death. For the bereaved person the death was a tragedy and this view needs to be respected.

CHECKLIST

❏ I understand why self-help groups are especially relevant during times of grief.

❏ I understand the processes that we go through when we are grieving.

❏ I understand that grieving is a healthy, necessary process.

❏ I now know how to help those around me who are grieving.

Chapter 13

Ending loneliness

The aims of this chapter are to:

◆ examine the effects of loneliness;

◆ examine how we form friendships and bond with others; and

◆ identify methods of combating loneliness.

Loneliness

People say that you can be lonely even when you are in a crowd. A number of those in the *Retire 200* program had divorced or separated from unhappy marriages. Many commented that they had not realised how lonely they had been in their dysfunctional relationships until after their partnership had dissolved. Living with someone who is either perpetually morose or non-communicative can result in feelings of anxiety or depression similar to those experienced when loneliness is due to isolation.

Loneliness versus anxiety or depression

There is a growing body of evidence to suggest that many diagnoses of anxiety and depression are in fact predicated on the real underlying problem of loneliness. Some years ago, a study of stress among dentists concluded that many of them were suffering from the effects of 'professional isolation', or loneliness. The initial theory had suggested that the probable cause of dentists' stress levels was their constant association with anxious patients, however, it was eventually found that stress for this group of dentists was related to the fact that their 'best' work was performed in the company of a largely unappreciative audience. At the end of the day all the patient wanted was their teeth fixed with a minimum of pain. The fact that this feat was achieved through applying a technically difficult procedure was of little interest to them.

So how is the dilemma of dentists' stress relevant to those of us who are lonely? The issues are similar in that successes or achievements may go largely unrecognised and reinforced when we are alone. If we paint a room in the house or prepare an attractive garden bed the satisfaction gained may not seem quite the same if there is no one there to admire our achievements.

The psychological symptoms of loneliness

Loneliness occurs when people feel there is nobody with whom they can communicate intimately and openly on a regular basis. Lonely people report feeling bored, sad, nervous, worthless, powerless or absorbed with their own sense of emotional isolation. This problem is compounded because society reinforces the worth of people in relationships, so it is easy for those who are lonely to feel excluded from the mainstream of life. The subsequent feelings of isolation may then affect self-esteem and lead to feelings of hopelessness.

A common paradox occurs when lonely people become over-critical of others, blaming them for not making sufficient effort to rescue them from their loneliness. Consequently, some lonely people reject the well-intentioned approaches of others as being not good enough. If they persist in rejecting enough people for long enough, lonely people can set up a self-fulfilling prophecy that says, 'Because people don't really care that I am lonely and will not make sufficient effort to help me, I do not wish to interact with them.'

Such people may continue to remain lonely because of the impossibly high expectations they have about what constitutes friendship. Their demanding criteria may state that true friends should always be available and that true friends should always agree with their political, religious and social values. These criteria set some lonely people up for disappointment as new 'friendships' dissolve when unrealistic expectations fail to be realised.

Why we like others and why they like us

Knowing what it is that attracts you to others, and them to us, can be helpful when you are feeling wary about socialising again after a long period of loneliness. It is quite natural for your self-esteem to be a little ragged at this time; taking some of the mystery out of the bonding processes in friendship can give you the confidence you need to get started.

The following information, taken from social research, may help explain why some relationships have progressed the way they have, and why others have withered early.

Geographical location

Geographical location is relevant from four perspectives, namely, familiarity, availability, predictability and interaction.

Familiarity: The more familiar a person is, the more you find that you want to interact with them. Most people prefer to chat to people they know than to a stranger.

Availability: The nearer people live to each other, the higher the probability of them forming a relationship that may end up as a friendship. Studies of people living in large blocks of units have even shown that people form friendships more readily with their immediate neighbours than with residents living just a few units away.

Predictability: The better you know someone, the more likely you are to be able to predict how they will react in specific situations. This allows you to avoid accidentally annoying them with comments that may be in direct conflict with their beliefs. They, too, learn that you find certain behaviours annoying or offensive, and have the opportunity to avoid them as they build a friendship with you.

Interaction: Interacting with others on a regular basis increases the likelihood of forming a relationship with them. Social research indicates that where you have regular interactions with a person, you will look for evidence to convince yourself that they are interesting, intelligent or special in some way.

Physical/personal attributes

Physical attractiveness: It seems that attractive people do have an easier time making friends, particularly during the early stages of friendship. One study some years ago even showed that highly attractive people 'sound' good-looking on the telephone! However, if like most of us you are not a raving beauty, do not despair! Social research provides two reassuring facts:

- Studies of couples in long-term relationships indicate that people usually pair up with those who are about equal to them on perceived attractiveness.

- For relationships to endure, other aspects such as commonality of interests, general politeness and pleasantness are more important than good looks.

Warmth: People like to be around those who have a warm personality. From a psychological perspective, 'warmth' relates to the tendency of people to rate other people and events positively rather than negatively. It also includes being accepting of others rather than being aloof or overcritical. Consequently, those who usually see the positive aspects of people are more appealing to us than those whose typical attitude is to find fault.

Apart from the congenial atmosphere surrounding warm people, their general air of approval encourages those around them to self-disclose in a safe environment. This is an important personal attribute because being able to safely self-disclose is one of the key risk-taking behaviours intrinsic to the relationships of close friends.

The halo effect: The halo effect describes the tendency to rate people highly if you find them attractive, or gifted in one particular area of their make-up. For example, a person who loves classical music may highly rate the overall worth of a person who is an authority on music even though they may have a number of unpleasant aspects to their personality. Similarly, the halo effect operates where a neat, well-dressed person is regarded as more intelligent or more capable than their untidy, overweight colleague even though there is no factual basis for this assessment.

The relevance of the halo effect to making new friends is simply that you tend to bond most easily with those that you consider competent in areas you regard as important. Once you identify an aspect of a new acquaintance's make-up or values that aligns closely with your own you are more likely to regard them favourably. One man told of moving into a new neighbourhood shortly after retiring. His next door neighbour was fastidious in the way he maintained his garden and came over to introduce himself simply because the new arrival mowed the lawn the day after moving in!

Commonality: Given the choice, people prefer to be in the company of those with similar attitudes to their own. When you are with people who see life the way you do, your own values are reinforced and you feel good about yourself. Consequently, people of a particular culture, religion or sporting interest will find that they are more comfortable in the company of others with like preferences or views.

Ways to manage loneliness

Strategies for dealing with loneliness

No one strategy for dealing with loneliness will suit all people. Everyone varies in the way they socialise, in their levels of self-confidence and in the types of activities they find enjoyable. If loneliness is an ongoing problem for you, assess how you are performing in relation to your attitudes, your skills and your behaviours.

The following section examines those aspects of behaviours that can help smooth the way for you as you start to form new friendships.

Your attitudes:

Ask yourself these questions and try to answer them as honestly as you can. Where you detect some attitudes that can be improved, put in some work on them.

Are you equating 'being alone' with 'loneliness'? We all need some time alone to read books, to think about life and to plan. In fact, not having enough time alone can be a major source of stress. It is only when you find that you are alone too often for your own liking that you become lonely.

Do you set unrealistically high criteria for how you expect your family and friends to behave towards you? Are you demanding that family and friends are always there for you regardless of their own needs and schedules? Do you define loyalty and friendship in black and white terms where people 'must' behave according to your standards at all times?

If you set unrealistically high standards for other people's behaviour you are heading for disappointment. It is rare indeed to find a friend whose values will always be the same as yours in every aspect of life. For example, I have a friend who I know would be there for me under any circumstances. I have another friend who makes me laugh more than anyone I know yet in a time of need would probably run in the opposite direction. Our friendship is based not on dependability or loyalty, but rather on our keen mutual sense of the ridiculous.

Do you blame others for your unhappiness? For example, when an acquaintance stops making contact as regularly as they used to it may just be that the relationship has run its course or that there are no longer sufficient areas of mutual interest to keep it alive. It also can be that their own lives are full and they are flat out dealing with their own responsibilities. When this occurs it is usually no one person's fault and you do not need to attribute blame to yourself or to them.

Are you becoming self-centred? It is very easy for lonely people to spend too much time dwelling on their own predicament. Apart from causing themselves unnecessary anxiety and depression, they can become painfully self-centred—which exacerbates their problems in finding new social contacts.

When you start meeting people after a period of loneliness try to avoid the temptation to pour out all of the worries and concerns that you have been storing up. Listening to the problems of established friends is one thing; having to listen to those of a new acquaintance will usually send people scurrying for cover.

Your skills

Do you lack the necessary social skills when forming new relationships? Facing new social situations can be daunting for some people even when all is going well in their lives. Where loneliness has been a persistent problem, it may signal that assertiveness skills require practice so that the difficult first steps can be taken to establish social contacts. Chapter 3 provides ideas if using assertive behaviour is a problem for you.

Do you communicate effectively with others? An excellent way to start relating with someone that you have just met is to quickly demonstrate to them that you are a good listener. Chapter 2 provides specific ways of improving interpersonal communication skills; for now, however, the following points may be helpful.

- When first meeting someone that you are interested in getting to know better, make a determined effort to listen closely to them.

- Demonstrate that you are listening by periodically feeding back the content of what they have said, and asking questions. By following up with a question, you demonstrate that you have been tuned in to what they are saying. You are then more likely to hold their interest than if you try to impress them by talking about yourself.

Your behaviours

Overcoming loneliness takes determination and action. People will not usually beat a path to your door to rescue you from your plight so it is up to you to start the ball rolling. Take the following steps to start combating loneliness.

Make a list of new places to go. If you go to new places, you are more likely to meet new people. The range of places you can go to meet people is virtually limitless. You can join clubs, enrol in courses, go to free concerts in parks, attend art exhibitions, flower shows—anywhere where you have the opportunity to start a casual conversation with people in a safe, friendly environment.

Another benefit associated with moving out of your usual territory is that it is much easier to approach strangers when you are not in your own neighbourhood. For example, people who would normally find it difficult to approach strangers will do so with comparative ease when asking for directions in a strange city. Having such an 'excuse' to speak with others removes a lot of the self-consciousness we may be feeling.

Opening a conversation. As you mingle at functions, look around the group for people you think you may like. Open a casual conversation with them about something relevant. For example, 'That's a beautiful painting isn't it!' or 'Have you been on one of these courses before?'

Of course, not all of the people you approach will wish to chat. They may have come there to relax, or may be so absorbed by the event that they wish to focus their attention on it. It is important that you understand their needs and that you try not to interpret their reluctance to talk as a personal rejection. At times, you may find that the ratio of initial approaches to ongoing conversations is quite low. However, in the meantime you have pushed your loneliness to one side as you courageously empowered yourself by mixing with other people. Moreover, each approach has brought you one step closer to meeting someone with whom you can form a friendship or spend some time.

Managing anxiety. When you enter a new social environment it is easy to interpret the anticipation you are feeling as anxiety. Paradoxically, the symptoms of anxiety can be much the same as the feelings you get when you are anticipating something pleasant. For example, on the morning of leaving for a long-awaited overseas holiday, people may awaken with butterflies in the stomach, an elevated pulse rate and sweaty palms. Yet these are the same symptoms that you experience during an attack of anxiety. It is therefore important to remind yourself that if you experience such feelings in new social situations it is quite normal.

If you find that anxiety does become a problem during your encounters, refer to Chapter 10 where you will find some techniques to help you relax at these times.

Taking the initial conversation a step further. After talking for a while with a new person you may wish to take the relationship to the next level by suggesting a further meeting. Gauge the situation before deciding how you are going to take the next steps. For example, if you are a man and the other person is a woman, suggest meeting for a cup of coffee or lunch somewhere on neutral territory such as a restaurant or coffee shop. The important thing to remember is that the other person needs to feel safe and that they can 'escape' easily if things do not go well.

Ending loneliness

Help other lonely people

When you are lonely it is easy for you to focus on your own dilemmas, which usually does little to improve your situation. Consider providing company and assistance to other lonely people. By focusing on others, you will find that you begin to forget your own problems and there is certainly no shortage of people to help! If this idea appeals to you, try contacting a few charities and offering your services.

Stay involved

Happy people are rarely idle—they stay involved and are usually prepared to try new ideas. Try doing something you have never done before just for the fun of it. For example, if there is a subject you hold strong views about write a few letters to the papers about it and see if they are published.

Escapism—taking the easy way out

When you are lonely or depressed you may find yourself spending a lot of time sleeping. The problem with this is that too much sleep can just be an escape from problems or miseries that are still there when you wake up. Moreover, spending too much time in bed can be physically detrimental as muscles atrophy, resulting in weakness. One answer to this problem is to set a schedule of rising at the same time each day as if you were going to work, a technique that was used by several of the participants in the research program. Also, make sure that you schedule tasks for yourself during the day and avoid other escapes such as watching too much television or abusing alcohol or drugs.

Stay involved with your community

Find ways of connecting with the rest of your community. If you find the prospect of joining community organisations a little daunting, try starting by just attending as an interested observer. Council meetings and lobby groups are a good place to start as they usually welcome observers.

Join a club or group

Check with your community office or the Yellow Pages to compile a list of groups or clubs to join. You will be surprised at the range of activities that are available. Even if none of these appeals to you, the process of looking may help you generate other ideas for activities, such as short courses at local schools or colleges.

Moving from planning to action

You may have read the preceding pages and have felt that there were some ideas there that you could put into action. If you did then you are off to a great start. However, if you have been lonely for some time, or if your loneliness has resulted from the end of a long relationship or marriage, you may find that you require some motivation to get going. A good way to achieve momentum in such situations is to draw up an action plan of goals.

Action plans do not have to be elaborate. In fact, the clearer and easier they are to write and maintain, the more likely you are to actually use them! The following action plan will ensure that you maximise the likelihood of meeting new friends or acquaintances. You may wish to use it as it is or, preferably, adapt it to meet your own needs and circumstances.

Sunday evening

Go through the weekend papers and the local weekly paper and search for advertisements, notices or articles about free or interesting events such as art shows, concerts, openings and book readings.

Every day

Keep a notebook or sheet of paper in your purse or wallet and write down the details of coming events that you see advertised in your daily trips to the shops or elsewhere.

Set up a planner

Get a diary or wall calendar in which to record the times and venues of all the events you have found in your search. Fill your week with as many potential events as possible.

Act!

Up until now, it has been an academic exercise. Now is the time for action. Decide which of the events you are going to attend and make sure that you go. Be courageous—do not put it off! DO IT!

CHECKLIST

❑ I have examined the list of attitudes, skills and behaviours required to form new friendships and will take action to improve my social skills where this is necessary.

❑ I have designed my own action plan to ensure that I attend sufficient social occasions each week.

SECTION V:

The impact of personality and the need to cross skill

Gaining insight into how your personality and those of your partner and friends affects your lives can be a valuable experience. People who explore why they react the way they do in certain situations often describe a profound sense of relief at what they discover. They may learn, for example, that their own lack of success in a particular area is not because they are dumb or lazy, rather it is because the area concerned is not one where they naturally focus their attention. Similarly, people in relationships discover why it is that their partner reacts differently from themselves in some situations and not others. Such insight can remove a sense of irritation that may have been present in the relationship for years.

In Chapter 15 the need for partners to cross skill so that both individuals can perform all roles and responsibilities presently shared between them are examined.

Chapter 14

How personality affects your life in retirement

The aims of this chapter are to:

◆ discover how people of different personality types view the world;

◆ learn how your personality impacts on your adjustment to life in retirement; and

◆ identify your own personality style so that you can take steps to improve your level of satisfaction with life.

What is personality?

There are countless explanations and definitions of personality, and arriving at one definition that is universally accepted is well nigh impossible. However, American psychologist and writer Christopher Monte wrote that when we are examining personality we are essentially 'looking at human nature'.

This chapter examines a model of personality developed by Carl Jung and later refined by Isabel Myers and Katherine Briggs. The resulting model of personality has become one of the most widely known around the world and is used in counselling, personal development and in organisational settings. When psychologists are determining where an individual fits in this model of personality, they use a personality assessment instrument known as the Myers-Briggs Type Indicator® or MBTI®.

Personality and relationships

The old saying 'opposites attract' appears to be true when it comes to the choice of your partner. In a study conducted some years ago, the personality types of a large group of couples were measured using the Myers-Briggs Type Indicator®. Of the couples surveyed, 91 per cent comprised partnerships where the personality type of each individual was different.

The evidence seems to suggest that opposites often attract in the early stages of a relationship. However, the daily process of then effectively interacting with each other in a constructive and stress-free manner is made more difficult where significant personality differences are present. The wider the differences, the more likely it is that couples will not see eye to eye on matters affecting the stability of their relationship.

However, if both people in a relationship understand *why* they each prefer to act as they do, it can go a long way to reducing stress. It also allows both partners to focus on the benefits that each brings to the relationship. This can be particularly important during retirement when you and your partner are going to be spending more time together than when you were working.

Of course, personality affects more than just the interactions of those in a relationship. Understanding your personality style can help explain why it is that, in certain situations, you seem to feel ill at ease or to experience stress and discomfort. Just as important is understanding why you excel in other situations, so that you can capitalise on them. Similarly, having a basic understanding of the structure of personality can help you understand why others around you react to situations in the way they do.

Jung, Myers and Briggs

There have been countless books written about the personality scales developed by Jung, Myers and Briggs. If you find that your interest in the area of personality grows as a result of reading this chapter, there are some references for further reading at the end of the book. In the meantime, what follows is a simplified explanation of the elements of the Myers-Briggs model. As you proceed, you will find ways of applying these elements to your life.

The four sub-scales

There are four sub-scales of the Myers-Briggs model that classify your personality:

Extraversion (E), which is the opposite of Introversion (I).

Sensing (S), which is the opposite of Intuition (N).

Thinking (T), which is the opposite of Feeling (F).

Judging (J) ,which is the opposite of Perceiving (P).

You will note that after each descriptor there is a letter in brackets— these are used for convenience when discussing the Myers-Briggs model. When people complete the Myers-Briggs Type Indicator® their 'type' is expressed as a combination of four of these letters to help them remember their classification.

When personality is classified using the Myers-Briggs model we refer to their 'personality *preferences*' is used. For example, on the MBTI® I am an ENTP, which means my personality preferences are Extraversion, Intuition, Thinking and Perception. There is a very good reason for using the term 'preferences'. Carl Jung, Katharine Briggs and Isabel Myers expressed their concept of personality in terms of people's preferences rather than in terms of them having fixed traits or skills. This indicates that you are therefore quite capable of accessing your less preferred personality dimensions and are not locked into always behaving in the same way. The important topic of 'preferences' is discussed in more detail later in the chapter.

Each personality preference, whether it be Extraversion versus Introversion, or Thinking versus Feeling, brings with it special gifts and insights that compliment those of people with different preferences. No single personality style is better than any other. Isabel Myers summed up this premise through the clever title of her book on the MBTI®, *Gifts Differing.*

Extraversion (E) versus Introversion (I)

The first sub-scale is Extraversion versus Introversion. This sub-scale describes the way you orient yourself to the rest of the world. It measures whether you are more interested in the outer world of people and things (Extraversion) or the inner world of concepts and ideas (Introversion).

Sometimes, people have gained the incorrect perception that being Extraverted is in some way better than being Introverted. For example, you will often hear people saying something like, 'Fred is a fantastic bloke—he's a real extravert!' In fact, extraverted behaviour is highly desirable in some circumstances, for example when chairing the meeting of your social club, however, introverted behaviour is highly desirable in others, for example, spending several quiet hours bringing the financial records of your social club up to date. This is not to suggest that the Introvert could not chair the meeting, or that the Extravert could not focus on the lonely job of working on the club's records. It is just that Extraverts will often *prefer* tasks involving interaction with people, and Introverts will often *prefer* tasks where they can quietly focus.

Consequently, a research scientist whose job requires them to work quietly in a back room for months at a time may find this task easier as an Introvert than as an Extravert. Highly Extraverted scientists would forever want to walk around and talk to people! On the other hand, the research scientist who needs to address the media to announce an exciting breakthrough would probably feel more comfortable performing this public role as an Extravert than as an Introvert.

The table below illustrates some of the differences between Extraverts and Introverts. As you read it, ask yourself which one of the two columns best describes your preferences!

EXTRAVERSION (E)	INTROVERSION (I)
Do not mind interruptions to their work	Do not like interruptions when working
Breadth, action and variety	Depth, quiet concentration
A lot	A few
Find meeting new people is more stimulating and interesting than tiring and draining	Find meeting new people more tiring and draining than stimulating and interesting
May prefer mixing with a wide range of people	May prefer the close friendship of a few people than mixing with a wide range of people
May put social life before private life	Value their private life before their social life
May prefer to join in the hurly-burly of a group discussion than to speak quietly with one person	May prefer to speak quietly with one person than to join in the hurly-burly of a group discussion
People, things	Ideas, quiet thinking
Prefer action and change and may act on the spur of the moment	Do not mind focusing on the one task for considerable periods of time
Prefer to work with a lot of other people around	Prefer to work with fewer people around
Sometimes act before they think	More likely to think first, then act
Would rather discuss a topic with someone than to quietly reflect on it	Think before taking action and tend to reflect on ideas before discussing them with others

Sensing (S) versus Intuition (N)

The second sub-scale of the Myers-Briggs model describes the way you prefer to take in information from the world around you. Do you see things accurately by applying your five senses to see detail (S), or do you prefer to look for possibilities and meaning by focusing more on the global picture (N)?

SENSING (S)	INTUITION (N)
Are often more interested in measurable and tangible facts than in abstract theories and possibilities	Are often more interested in abstract theories and possibilities than in measurable and tangible facts
Believe it is better to apply existing processes based on experience than to try theories and predictions	Believe theories and predictions of what could be are more interesting than using existing processes based on experience
Common sense	Imagination
Decisions may be based on experience	Decisions may be based on a hunch
Described as practical and down to earth rather than as dreamers of new ideas or concepts	Described as dreamers of new ideas or concepts rather than as practical and down to earth
Fine detail—accuracy	Overview—big picture
Have a good eye for detail and are good at picking flaws in a design, a piece of art etc.	View the world in a global way and may fail to see detail such as an important number buried in a detailed profit and loss statement
Now, facts, reality	Future, possibility, dreams
Often regarded as more predictable than innovative	Often regarded as more innovative than predictable
Sometimes described as living in the 'here and now', using their five senses to take in information accurately	Prefer to put a more global interpretation on what they see and look for the overall picture
May be seen more as realistic than imaginative	May be seen more as imaginative than realistic

Those with a Sensing preference are more likely to rely on past experience as their most highly valued basis for arriving at decisions. Intuitives on the other hand tend to look more for what possibilities the future holds for them. While those who are Sensing are sometimes described as realistic or 'grounded' and living in the real world, Intuitives are more likely to look forward to change and to events in the future.

Thinking (T) versus Feeling (F)

The third sub-scale of the Myers-Briggs model relates to opposite ways of arriving at decisions. The labels 'Thinking' and 'Feeling' do not mean to imply that those with a Feeling preference do not think, or that those with a Thinking preference are incapable of feeling! Rather, the labels indicate that *when it comes to making decisions*, people with the Thinking preference are more likely to rely on objective logic and will be influenced mostly by facts, while those with the Feeling preference will prefer to make decisions where the outcomes are less likely to affect others adversely.

It should also be emphasised that both Feeling and Thinking people can react with similar levels of emotional intensity; it is just that those with the Feeling preference tend to display their emotions more openly. Sometimes such open displays can be a problem for any Ts that happen to be around at the time—they may find themselves becoming embarrassed by what they see as inappropriate or excessive displays of emotion.

THINKING (T)	FEELING (F)
Are described more often as rational than obeying their heart when making decisions	Are seen as more often obeying their heart than their head when making decisions
Are more likely to be seen as firm and decisive rather than compassionate	Are more likely to be seen as warm and compassionate rather than firm and decisive
Are more likely to be seen as logical and clear thinking than as concerned about others' feelings	Are more likely to be seen as concerned about others' feelings than as logical or objective
Intellect, justice	Emotion, humanity
Look for facts that are clear and measurable to build their case when arguing a point	Tend to use persuasion rather than logic when trying to win an argument
Prefer to identify what has gone wrong than to provide sympathy and comfort	Prefer to provide sympathy and comfort than to identify what has gone wrong

Tend to rely on logic and objectivity when making decisions	Are more likely to make decisions based on the impact they will have on other people
When they see situations where people are not performing well at a task, they find it comparatively easy to tell them where they are going wrong	When they see situations where people are not performing well at a task, they may find it difficult to tell them where they are going wrong

Judging (J) versus Perceiving (P)

The fourth sub-scale relates to the way you put your decisions into action. Those with the Judging preference are keen to act on decisions as soon as possible and have what some people have described as a 'high need for closure'. Perceptives on the other hand may feel pressured by a tight deadline, arguing that they need time to gather more information before they act just in case there is some important issue that has not yet been considered.

PERCEIVING (P)	JUDGING (J)
Are more comfortable with change and spontaneity	Are more comfortable with a routine that is predictable
Even if they are working to an agreed plan or schedule, changes along the way make the otherwise predictable routine more interesting	If they are working to an agreed plan or schedule, they dislike changes along the way
Have a flexible schedule	Keep to a fixed schedule
Having daily plans to stick to restricts them too much	Not knowing what their plans are makes them uneasy until they have a plan in place
Keep options open	Work to plan
Let life happen, adapt, keep exploring	Manage life, plan, decide
Prefer to keep options open	Wish to get things completed as soon as possible
Spontaneous, play, adventure	Controlled, work, order

Tend to get very enthusiastic at the start of projects but become bored when it comes to putting on the finishing touches	Tend to work steadily during projects from start to finish
When a decision has been made they may become restless and worry that they should have obtained more information before making the decision	Take deadlines very seriously and will be disappointed if others do not do likewise
Would rather let life unfold than stick to predictable schedules or plans	Would rather stick to predictable schedules or plans than just let life unfold

Your personality type

The most accurate way to discover your personality type is to complete the Myers-Briggs Type Indicator® which, in Australia, is licensed by Consulting Psychologists Press. Only a psychologist or other suitably qualified person can administer the MBTI®. If you find the personality concepts described in this chapter interesting and would like to use them for your personal development, then arranging to complete the Myers-Briggs Type Indicator® is recommended.

In the meantime, you can continue to learn more about your personality preferences by going back now and re-reading the descriptions of the pairs of sentences in the four tables above. As you examine each pair of sentences, you will find that the phrases in one column of each pair appear to describe your behaviour more accurately than the sentences in the other column. For example, the list of points describing an Introvert may sound more like you than the list describing an Extravert. If so, then it is more likely that you are an Introvert (I) than an Extravert (E).

Go through each of the four pairs of lists and see if you can decide which of each of the pairs best describes you. In the boxes below, write down the four letters (E or I, S or N, F or T and J or P) which best represent your personality style so that you then have a set of four letters. When you have finished:

◆ The first box on the left should have either an E or an I in it.

◆ The second box should have either an N or an S in it.

◆ The third box should have either a T or an F in it.

◆ The last box on the right should have either a P or a J in it.

Your calculation of your personality preferences.

Remember that without completing the Myers-Briggs Type Indicator® itself you should only use the above method as a rough assessment.

Some of the descriptions in your columns may not seem to match your personality because as an individual you report the strength of your preferences on each of the scales in varying degrees. For example, if you are an Extravert, you will probably find that some of the statements describing an Extravert apply to you but others seem to miss the mark.   Below are the scores of two Extraverts who have completed the Myers-Briggs Type Indicator®. As you can see Extravert (B) has a strong score on Extraversion while Extravert (A) scores low. The Extravert with the low score (3) may have found that their score on Extraversion was only marginally higher than their score on Introversion. On the other hand, the Extravert with the high score (45) would probably have found that *most* of the descriptors in the Extravert column were relevant to him/her.

Extravert A (Low score = 3)

EXTRAVERSION −|−|−|−|−|−|−↓|−|−|−|−|−|−|− INTROVERSION
60 50 40 30 20 10 0 10 20 30 40 50 60

Extravert B (High score = 45)

EXTRAVERSION −|−|−↓|−|−|−|−|−|−|−|−|−|−|− INTROVERSION
60 50 40 30 20 10 0 10 20 30 40 50 60

The fact that the Myers-Briggs model accommodates different levels of strengths in each sub-scale is often a great relief to those people who would otherwise resent being pigeonholed into one of sixteen identical and inflexible personality types.

If you are interested in exploring the effect of the strength of your own personality preferences there are a number of texts on the MBTI® available in larger or specialist bookshops. Most university libraries also have texts on the Myers-Briggs model and you usually do not have to be an enrolled student to use the library as a non-borrower.

When you consider the various sub-scales of the Myers-Briggs model it is also important to remember that you are looking at your *preferences* for behaving or for making decisions, not at your *skills*. Consequently, an Introvert can use extraverting behaviours if they need to, and an Extravert can use introverting behaviours. In fact, during every day of our lives we access both our preferred and our less preferred personality styles. For example, although I am an Extravert, the processes involved in writing this book required far more introverting behaviours than extraverting behaviours.

The table shows the behaviours that were needed to write this book.

Introverting behaviours (I)	Extraverting behaviours (E)
Design methodology for the research program in which the retirement experiences of 200 retirees were examined *(50+ hours)*	Discuss research design with university staff *(12+ hours)* Interview 200 retirees *(200+ hours)*
Collate and process the data of 200 retirees *(300+ hours)*	Discuss the proposed book with the publisher *(3+ hours)*
Statistically analyse data and draw conclusions *(60+ hours)*	Speak at publisher's marketing meeting *(1+ hours)*
Write research paper *(800+ hours)*	Attend book launch *(2 hours)*
Write the book *(2000+ hours)*	
Total Introverting hours = 3210+	**Total Extraverting hours = 218+**

Applying knowledge of personality preferences
Your personality and life in retirement

This section looks at how aspects of personality affect your life in retirement.

If you are an Extravert (E)

◆ You will need to ensure that you are involved in a sufficiently wide range of activities to provide you with variety. This is important if you are to remain challenged and stimulated.

◆ You will need to ensure that your activities allow sufficient opportunities to interact with groups of people rather than just comprising quiet, solitary tasks.

◆ Extraverts are known for their tendency to act quickly, sometimes without thinking matters through carefully enough. While this can make Extraverts exciting to be around, they need to be careful that their natural tendency to action does not bring them undone when making important financial decisions.

◆ Extraverts enjoy the cut and thrust of debate. Consequently, they can be vulnerable to the exciting, lively sales talk of entrepreneurs with 'get rich quick' schemes. This fact is probably behind the old saying, 'The easiest person to sell to is another salesperson.' Therefore, Extraverts need to remind themselves that in retirement, they will not have the earning capacity to recover from heavy losses resulting from hastily considered financial decisions.

If you are an Introvert (I)

◆ Introverts lean towards activities that require quiet involvement and will often enjoy participating in projects that require prolonged, focused attention.

◆ Introverts prefer to communicate on a one-to-one basis, or in small groups of people that they know well. Given the choice, some Introverts may prefer that communication be written rather than oral.

◆ Introverts are less likely than Extraverts to react quickly or to rush into decisions. However, they need to ensure that they do not allow their tendency to think before they act to freeze them into inaction.

If you are of the Sensing (S) preference

◆ Those with the Sensing preference will usually prefer to become involved in activities that are practical and which have measurable, observable outcomes.

◆ Sensing people usually prefer to use the skills they have already developed than to learn new ones. It is therefore likely that they will prefer activities where they apply skills that were acquired before they retired.

If you are an Intuitive (N)

◆ When looking for activities, Intuitives should consider including study or short courses. This is because they gain pleasure from acquiring new skills or knowledge.

◆ Intuitives are usually interested in solving new or complex problems.

◆ Intuitives use of imagination and insight will often act as a catalyst for constructive discussion among other members of groups such as committees.

If you are of the Thinking (T) preference

◆ When people with the Thinking preference are seeking activities, they may be more comfortable in roles where they need to apply logic rather than dealing with the emotional problems of others.

◆ Where committee work is involved, the tough-mindedness of those with the Thinking preference will be important. However, they need to be careful that they do not react too impersonally, thereby hurting others feelings in the process.

◆ When it comes to financial decisions those with the Thinking preference will be more likely to apply cool, analytical solutions to decision-making. While this is a valuable approach when it comes to financial decision-making, they will need to check that their partner is also happy with the proposed outcomes.

If you are of the Feeling (F) preference

◆ When those with the Feeling preference are making important decisions, they will tend to be influenced more by their values than by the logical outcome that the cold hard facts may suggest.

◆ Because of their desire to please others, those with the Feeling preference may find it difficult to break bad news or to provide critical opinions to others even when it is required.

If you are of the Judging (J) preference

◆ Those with the Judging preference will usually prefer activities that involve a reasonably high level of structure.

◆ Once a plan of action is decided those with the Judging preference usually dislike changes along the way, preferring to stick to their original plan.

◆ In committees, Judging people are likely to focus on the milestone dates that tasks need to be completed by, because they are driven by their need to bring projects to closure.

If you are of the Perceiving (P) preference

◆ Those with a Perceiving preference will most likely enjoy activities involving change or flexibility from rigid schedules.

◆ Where it is important that an activity or project is completed on time, Perceptives will need to be careful that they do not keep postponing the completion of tasks because they *need* more information.

◆ Because they like change, Perceptives will need to ensure that the activities they seek do not involve too much routine or repetition.

Optimising the benefits of your personality style

As mentioned earlier, the Myers-Briggs model of personality is based on your *preferences* for acting. The word 'preferences' is very important because it emphasises the fact that you have the ability to modify your preferred behaviour when you need to. Therefore, instead of describing your preferences in terms of your strengths and weaknesses, it is more helpful to view them as your 'developed' and 'less developed' preferences for acting.

Perceptives, for example, are not likely to have a natural preference for planning or scheduling. This may lead them to go through life believing that they do not have the skills or discipline to plan. Yet, once they are aware that their natural preference is not to plan, they can then make the decision to plan meticulously if required.

'Mapping' personality preferences to improve performance

Mapping involves identifying all the actions that comprise a task and then checking them off against your own personality preferences. Where you then find that a particular task or aspect of a task does not match your particular preferences, you simply make a note to take special care during this phase of your activity. For example, if you are an Intuitive (N) but the task requires attention to fine detail, you can simply make a conscious decision to focus carefully during this phase of the task.

You can map your preferences against the tasks you have to complete or the decisions you need to make by using the following process:

1. Ensure you are familiar with the descriptions of your personality preferences.

2. Ask yourself, 'What personality attributes does this task or decision seem to require?':

   (i)   Does the task or decision require quiet concentration for prolonged periods of time (Introverting behaviour), or does it need someone to promote concepts/ideas to others or to interact with groups of people (Extraverting behaviour)?

   (ii)   Does the task or decision require accuracy or attention to fine detail (Sensing behaviour), or does it require a vision of how to do things differentially from the way they have been done in the past (Intuiting behaviour)?

   (iii) Does the task or decision require an objective, logical approach or the implementation of tough decisions (Thinking behaviour), or does it require you to focus on the personal impacts of decisions on others (Feeling behaviour)?

(iv) Does the task or decision require spontaneous behaviour with many changes and new inputs along the way (Perceiving behaviour), or does it require working to a detailed plan or schedule where meeting agreed timetables is important (Judging behaviour)?

3. Having identified and listed the personality attributes required to successfully perform the task, ask yourself, 'Which of these are NOT found among my personality preferences?' Review the personality variables described earlier and make a list of the *less* preferred areas of your personality (those of the opposite letters to yours), that are important to successfully performing the task or making the decision.

4. Finally, now that you have identified the personality attributes that were NOT found among your personality preferences, make a list of them and keep them close by for the duration of the task or decision-making process. If, for example, you need to focus for long periods by yourself, but as an Extravert prefer to mix with others, say to yourself, 'It is important that I remain focused during this time. Therefore while I would dearly like to get up and engage people in conversation, I will use self-discipline and remain quietly focused for as long as I need to be in order to complete the task.' Similarly, if you are an Intuitive and the task requires attention to detail, say to yourself, 'While my tendency is to skim pages looking for broad trends, I will discipline myself to check each figure carefully. I CAN do this even if I do find it irksome!'

Personalities and relationships

The following section looks at relationship issues that may arise due to the interaction of particular personality styles. Understanding where your respective personalities are aligned and where they differ will allow you to better appreciate the attributes you share in common. Conversely, through insight and understanding you are more likely to be understanding of your partner's personality preferences where they differ from or clash with your own.

Both of us are Extraverts (E)

Aspects of our personality where we complement each other

We both enjoy socialising and entertaining.

We find it easy to discuss issues that are concerning us.

We like to keep busy by having a number of activities on the go at once.

Aspects of our personalities that require monitoring

Because we both like talking and interacting, we may not listen carefully enough to each other.

Our levels of activity are high but we need to ensure that we share some activities so that we spend enough time together.

We need to ensure that in accommodating each other's need for action, we set aside some time for individual reflection and thought.

One of us is an Extravert (E) and the other is an Introvert (I)

Aspects of our personality where we complement each other

The outgoing Extravert takes pressure off the Introvert to 'perform' at social occasions.

The Introvert enjoys listening to the Extravert, who in turn enjoys talking.

Aspects of our personalities that require monitoring

When we are both suffering from stress, the Introvert needs peace and solitude to recover while the Extravert may prefer to surround themselves with people.

The Extravert's enthusiastic, outgoing personality is balanced by the Introvert's quieter, calmer personality.

When we have a major problem to solve together, the Extravert will want to discuss it with the Introvert so that they can work out the problem together. However, the Introvert will prefer to solve the problem alone first and then discuss the solution he/she has generated.

The Introvert wants more privacy and time alone than the Extravert who may have difficulty in understanding this need for solitude and contemplation.

We are both Introverts (I)

Aspects of our personality where we complement each other

We enjoy quiet times alone together or with small groups of people who we know well.

We understand each other's need for privacy and time alone.

We can be in the same room together for hours without feeling the need to keep a conversation going or to attend to each other.

Aspects of our personalities that require monitoring

We find that providing negative feedback to each other is difficult. This may mean that we bottle up issues for too long until they blow out of proportion.

Because we do not discuss important issues as often as we should, we may wrongly assume that our actions meet with our partner's approval.

We risk becoming too isolated from others due to our contentment with our own company.

We are both Sensing (S)

Aspects of our personality where we complement each other

We do not overcomplicate our lives with mess and clutter.

We live in the here and now and do not waste time dreaming of a better future.

We do not cause ourselves stress through poor record keeping, for example, through forgetting to pay bills.

Aspects of our personalities that require monitoring

We may neglect to plan sufficiently for the future.

We may not try new ideas to solve recurring problems differently, thus limiting our ability to solve problems and move forward.

We may miss the opportunity to learn new skills due to our reliance on the methods we have used for years.

One of us is Sensing (S) and the other is Intuitive (N)

Aspects of our personality where we complement each other

The S is good at putting the N's ideas into action.

The S attends to important matters in the here and now, while the N thinks about new ideas for the future.

The N can help the S to appreciate abstract concepts, while the S can help the N keep their feet on the ground.

Aspects of our personalities that require monitoring

The N may irritate the S through their inattention to detail.

The S may irritate the N through insisting that they keep everything tidy.

When it comes to designing or decorating a residence, the S may focus on a practical design while the N may prefer a radical, less practical design.

We are both Intuitives (N)

Aspects of our personality where we compliment each other

We welcome change and new ways of doing things.

We find it easy to communicate with each other using theory and abstract concepts.

Aspects of our personalities that require monitoring

We may become stressed because we have too much going on in our lives at once.

While we are good at generating ideas we do not always bring them to fruition.

We may neglect the practical essentials of life such as maintaining the house and car and organising the orderly payment of bills.

We are both Thinking (T)

Aspects of our personality where we complement each other

We rarely offend each other because of poor communication.

We use logic to solve problems and do not become over emotional.

Aspects of our personalities that require monitoring

We may forget to say, 'I love you.'

We may find it difficult to attend to people's needs when they are visibly distressed.

We may have difficulty in showing our emotions.

One of us is Feeling (F) and the other is Thinking (T)

Aspects of our personality where we complement each other

The T finds it easier to be tough with people where this is required, and the F is more inclined to offer comfort and sympathy to those in distress.

The feelings and emotions of the F are balanced by the T's logical approach.

We complement each other with our objective (T) and subjective (F) views of the world.

Aspects of our personalities that require monitoring

When we are arguing, the T may offend the F with their cool, dispassionate logic.

The F wants peace and harmony while the T wants to resolve the problem.

Our public displays of intimacy are different, with the F being more demonstrable than the T.

We are both Feeling (F)

Aspects of our personality where we complement each other

We are both peacemakers and enjoy a harmonious relationship.

We consider each other's feelings and discuss issues to ensure that we both agree.

We genuinely like people.

Aspects of our personalities that require monitoring

We may overreact to personal criticism.

We may neglect our individual needs in our desire to please our partner.

We have trouble resolving conflict due to our strong need to please others and to maintain harmony.

We are both Judging (J)

Aspects of our personality where we complement each other

We reach decisions quickly.

We are both well organised and attend to our responsibilities with minimum fuss or procrastination.

We are both clear regarding the respective roles and responsibilities in our relationship.

Aspects of our personalities that require monitoring

Because we are so task-oriented we may leave too little time to relax and indulge ourselves.

Our need for plans and organisation may result in clashes because we both have strong convictions about how things should be done.

Because we both value 'closure' we may rush into important decisions without sufficient information to allow for an informed choice.

One of us is Judging (J) and the other is Perceptive (P)

Aspects of our personality where we complement each other

Our life is balanced between work (J) and play (P).

Our life is balanced between plans, structure and order (J) and spontaneous fun (P).

Aspects of our personalities that require monitoring

The J may see the P as too fun loving and the P may see the J as too serious.

We arrive at decisions differently because the J desires closure and the P wants to delay closure to gain more information.

Household maintenance is important to the J and avoided by the P.

We are both Perceiving (P)

Aspects of our personality where we complement each other	Aspects of our personalities that require monitoring
We enjoy change in our lives.	We may find that our house and car are poorly maintained.
We do not tie each other down with rigid schedules.	Important bills may be neglected until they have passed their due date.
We both enjoy fun times and ensure they form an important part of our lives.	Lack of order in our lives may bring unnecessary stress.

CHECKLIST

❑ I have read the descriptions of the four sub-scales of personality described and understand how each differs from its opposite preference, for example, Extraversion versus Introversion.

❑ I understand that I can use attributes of my opposite 'letter' because my type represents my *preferences,* not my skills.

❑ I have read the information on each sub-scale regarding its relevance to my retirement activities and pastimes.

❑ I understand how to map my personality preferences to perform better during important tasks or decisions.

❑ I know where the personality preferences of my partner and I complement each other, and which areas we need to monitor.

Chapter 15

Cross-skilling in relationships

The aims of this chapter are to:

◆ examine the need for partners to cross-skill;

◆ learn what participants on the *Retire 200* project reported about being over reliant on one partner; and

◆ identify key areas in which both partners should be competent.

The argument for cross-skilling

Research from recent sociological literature, and from the participants in *Retire 200* indicates that it is important for both partners in a relationship to be competent to perform the full range of duties that they manage collectively. Apart from issues relating to the fair distribution of responsibilities, it is important for both partners to know how to perform each other's roles for the following reasons:

◆ a partner can become ill or unable to perform heavy work due to complaints such as arthritis;

◆ a partner may pass away; or

◆ a partner may run away with Mr or Mrs Kafoops.

Clearly, any one of these scenarios is associated with significant stress. Acquiring a new skill when also suffering from stress or grief makes the learning process all that more difficult, particularly when the skill is far removed from your usual repertoire.

What are the outcomes of not cross-skilling? Consider these examples:

◆ Not knowing that it is important to check the temperature gauge in the car could result in a ruined engine costing several thousand dollars to replace.

◆ Not knowing that it is important to clean the lint filter on the clothes drier could result in your house burning down.

◆ Not understanding the basic workings of your investment portfolio could result in poor, costly decisions.

'Teach your husband to cook and wash so you can go out and do what you want!'

This participant had raised a large family in an older-style traditional household. Her husband's cooking skills were limited to the occasional weekend barbecue and he had never used the washing machine.

'When my wife left me it came out of the blue. I didn't even know how to cook and found myself going across the road each day to the take-away food shop and living on fried dim-sims and chicken and chips. I spent a fortune on dry cleaning because I didn't know how to iron a shirt. I think it was the food, and the stress of the break-up, that finally made me so ill.'

This man had moved from home as a young man where his mother had done all of his cooking and ironing straight into a marriage where his wife continued these roles. Consequently, when his wife left him a month before he retired he could not deal with the basics of cooking, or washing and ironing his clothes. He relied on take-away food for nearly a year and would probably still be doing so had not an old mate, horrified by his friend's helplessness, intervened and taught him the basics of cooking and ironing. (Once he had learned the basics of cooking, he became somewhat of a cooking enthusiast. When I spoke with him he was partway through a course on Chinese cooking and was loving every moment of it!)

'I was hospitalised for seven weeks and could not drive the car for another two months. During that time my wife had not known to check the pressure in the tyres. When I finally got around to it, three tyres were okay but one of the back tyres was practically flat.'

It is bad enough for someone to be forced to eat take-away food because they cannot cook. However, in this example the driver could have ended up in a serious accident.

'Sometimes she fires up the lawn mower while I prepare the evening meal or put a load of washing through. '

These husband and wife participants in our research had worked in demanding jobs for most of their lives, and owned a substantial home on a large block of land. When asked why they had cross-skilled, the husband indicated that they had initially started cross-skilling to take the load off each other whenever one of them was going through a particularly stressful time at work. After they retired, they felt secure knowing that if one of them became ill or died the other could still perform the essential functions of running the house and attending to responsibilities such as managing their investment portfolio.

'Some married women depend on their husbands too much—for example, some don't know how to write cheques, pay bills ...'

This woman described how her husband had become very ill and could not perform the basic roles he had looked after all their married life. She then found herself trying to learn new skills at this most stressful time.

Cross-skilling

Many of the following points were identified by the *Retire 200* program as areas in which both partners should be competent. You may think of more to add.

Area of expertise	Partner A	Partner B
Motor vehicles		
Knowing what the car's tyre pressure should be	❏	❏
Knowing how to check the tyre pressure	❏	❏

Area of expertise	Partner A	Partner B
Knowing how to inflate/deflate tyres to the correct pressure	❏	❏
Knowing how to check the car's oil and water	❏	❏
Knowing how to top up the car's oil and water (including windscreen washers)	❏	❏
Knowing what fuel the car takes (leaded/unleaded petrol, diesel, LP gas)	❏	❏
Knowing how to fill the car with fuel	❏	❏
Knowing what the gauges on the car's instrument panel mean and why it is necessary to keep a regular eye on them	❏	❏
Knowing to listen for unusual noises coming from the car and to immediately have them checked out by a mechanic	❏	❏
Knowing to have the car serviced according to the recommended maintenance schedule	❏	❏

Lawnmowers

	Partner A	Partner B
Knowing how to start *and* stop the mower	❏	❏
Knowing what fuel the mower takes (petrol or two stroke)	❏	❏
Knowing how to check the oil if it is a petrol mower	❏	❏
Knowing how to check the blades	❏	❏
Knowing to stop the mower before putting hands or feet near it or when emptying and replacing the grass catcher	❏	❏
Knowing to wear protective eye/ear/footwear when mowing	❏	❏
Knowing how often to get the mower serviced	❏	❏

Area of expertise	Partner A	Partner B
Shopping and cooking		
Knowing how to purchase the right food to ensure a healthy, balanced diet	❏	❏
Knowing how to buy and store food to maintain freshness and avoid waste	❏	❏
Knowing how to cook basic food items using methods such as steaming, roasting, grilling	❏	❏
Knowing how to use the basic functions of conventional and microwave ovens	❏	❏
Knowing how to clean conventional and microwave ovens	❏	❏
Washing and cleaning		
Knowing how to use a dishwasher including the use of correct detergents and rinse aid	❏	❏
Knowing what utensils must not be put in a dishwasher and what must be put on the top shelf only	❏	❏
Knowing how to use a clothes washing machine	❏	❏
Knowing how to use a clothes dryer	❏	❏
Knowing what clothes may and should not be put in washing machines and dryers	❏	❏
Knowing how to clean the filters of dishwashers, washing machines and clothes dryers (dirty lint filters in clothes dryers are a major cause of house fires)	❏	❏
Knowing what solvents and cleaners can and cannot be used on the various surfaces around the house (benches, tiles, wood, paint, plastic, leather, cork-tiles)	❏	❏
Knowing how to use an iron—set correct temperature, fill with water	❏	❏
Knowing how to iron clothes	❏	❏

Area of expertise	Partner A	Partner B
Using appliances		
Knowing how to set the time clocks on all time-based appliances—videos, microwaves, stoves, clocks, bedside radios	❏	❏
Knowing how to access the basic information stored on your home computer	❏	❏
Knowing how to use the basic functions of all electronic equipment in the home—radios, tape players, CDs, videos, TVs, vacuum cleaners	❏	❏
Knowing when and how to change vacuum cleaner bags	❏	❏
Knowing how to test the batteries in the smoke detector(s)	❏	❏
Knowing when and how to change the batteries in appliances such as smoke detectors, remote controls, radios, clocks	❏	❏
Knowing how to change a fuse	❏	❏
Knowing how to load and unload film in the camera	❏	❏
Finances		
Knowing how to manage your budget	❏	❏
Having a system for paying bills and filing receipts	❏	❏
Knowing how to complete your tax return or at least what records to maintain for your tax accountant	❏	❏
Knowing how to balance a cheque book	❏	❏
Understanding your share portfolio and how to best use the services of your stockbroker or financial adviser	❏	❏
Knowing how to access special benefits that are due to you (rebates, discounts relating to council rates, water, electricity, public transport etc.)	❏	❏

Area of expertise	Partner A	Partner B
Knowing what your social service entitlements are and how to access them	❏	❏
Knowing how to put into action advice provided by your financial adviser	❏	❏

Miscellaneous

	Partner A	Partner B
Knowing the range of council services that may be available, for example, moving heavy furniture	❏	❏
Having a list of reliable tradespeople	❏	❏

CHECKLIST

❏ I understand why it important for both partners to be competent across the range of tasks and responsibilities.

❏ We have examined the list of competencies and will begin to cross-skill where we find individual competency gaps.

SECTION VI:

Managing money and avoiding traps

The findings of the *Retire 200* program left little doubt that one of the most powerful factors influencing retirement-based anxiety, depression or stress related to being totally dependent on a government pension.

By the time that most people pick up this book, their retirement will probably be either well under way or just around the corner. Consequently, this next chapter does not address the wealth creation strategies typically found in books on superannuation or retirement planning. Rather, the chapter is included to suggest that people seek expert advice to maximise existing financial circumstances, and to alert readers to some of the expensive traps highlighted by those in our research program.

Chapter 16

Guarding your financial health

The aims of this chapter are to:

◆ identify potentially costly financial mistakes that can affect your life savings;

◆ identify criteria for use when seeking professional financial advice; and

◆ provide a format for calculating weekly, monthly and yearly costs of living

'In retirement you need twice as much money and half the clothes.'

The research found that financial matters, and in particular financial independence, rated among the top factors influencing well-being. Those people who were not financially independent tended to experience higher levels of anxiety, stress and depression than those who were financially independent.

Note: 'Financially independent' meant not depending solely on government pensions for one's income, that is, having an income from other sources such as superannuation or personal investments.

As the laws and regulations governing superannuation, retirement income streams and social security change so frequently, it is impossible for a book to provide other than very general information. Moreover, individual circumstances vary so widely that those seeking the answers to their retirement-related financial questions are wise to consult direct-ly with a qualified, trusted financial adviser.

Feedback

This section contains some of the observations of the participants in the Australian *Retire 200* program. Most of these people held strong views about superannuation, government pensions and how to manage their money. They were anxious to pass on these views for the benefit of others.

Living within your income

Those participants who were financially independent typically placed more importance on the security of their income than on the amount of income they received. As more than one participant said, 'I like to sleep at night!'

Usually, the more 'security conscious' a person was, the more likely they were to have taken an active interest in the accumulation of their retirement savings. Even where the majority of their retirement wealth accumulation was funded by superannuation, they could usually describe in some detail the investment portfolios that had comprised their superannuation plan.

At the 'collection' end of the superannuation savings years, security conscious retirees were also more likely than others to have both short-term budgets (for example, weekly living expenses) and medium-term budgets (for example, annual holidays, car registration). It seems that those who had taken an active personal interest in accumulating wealth over their working life are also the most interested in managing it well during their retirement years. Some of their observations include:

> 'Live within your means. Don't worry about others' ideas like always having the latest car. Don't have silly expectations.'

> 'You need enough money to be comfortable.'

> 'Financial security is important—you don't need a lot but you need to be comfortable.'

'Make sure that you have enough money to support your interests.'

The core message from these quotations appears to be, 'Look at your situation honestly and then resolve to live within your means.'

Getting the right advice

Younger retirees (aged 55 to 60) were more likely than their older counterparts to have sought advice from a financial adviser. Older retirees appeared to be more suspicious of financial advisers, preferring to manage their own finances or to use an accountant. This may be due to a lack of finance industry qualifications at the time older retirees were first planning for their retirement. Financial advisers and insurance brokers in Ireland are required to register with the Central Bank and meet minimum standards. That doesn't mean, of course, that they are all equally good or that they cannot give bad advice, but it does afford the consumer some protection.

When selecting a financial adviser, most participants indicated that they wanted someone who was competent and who understood their needs and circumstances. Importantly, they wanted to feel at ease with their adviser due to the private financial matters they would need to disclose to them (criteria to consider when selecting a financial adviser are discussed later in this chapter).

'Have a budget that you stick to—this will reduce stress over money worries.'

'Get a good accountant or financial adviser to explain investments to you.'

'Plan your finances before and after retiring.'

'Seek financial advice.'

It's never too late

'If you need money go out and make some.'

The above comment came from the participant who had set up a small business selling products out of the boot of his car at markets (see Chapter 1). He and a number of other participants demonstrated that it is possible to generate income in retirement without taking large financial risks, without necessarily investing large sums of money and without having special qualifications or experience.

Note: It is often possible for retirees to obtain part-time or casual employment without having to pay much tax. In Ireland there are generous tax exemption levels for the over 65s, and in the UK there are extra tax allowances. Similarly, such employment may not affect social welfare entitlement. Non-contributory social welfare benefits are means-tested but contributory pensions are paid irrespective of means in Ireland. As with most financial matters, always check with the relevant authorities to verify how such employment will affect your own circumstances.

Anxiety, depression and stress due to a lack of financial security

It was previously stated that the link between the psychological problems of anxiety, depression and stress and having insufficient financial resources was a significant finding in the research. In particular, stress caused by money worries was of great concern to many who regarded it as having a detrimental effect on their health. Even where financial problems were not an issue, most people could cite examples of friends or relatives who were 'finding it tough'.

'Go and have your finances checked out to have a stress-free retirement.'

'Understand your financial needs. Some people get very stressed over finances.'

'You need to have enough money to be worry free.'

'Plan your money details so that you do not have financial worries.'

'Beware when investing a lump sum. If you do not have a business mind you may invest in a catastrophe and lose the lot. I have seen many lose their money that way.'

'Your finances need to be sound for (i) security, and (ii) to be independent.'

'Financial stability and your health are important.'

To summarise, those who felt confident that their financial circumstances were secure were in better emotional shape than those who were constantly worried about money.

Living solely on the age pension

Managing solely on a social welfare pension challenged the ingenuity and creativity of most recipients. The very few who appeared to get by unscathed on the pension either had very simple, basic needs due to their lifestyle preferences or were receiving some other financial assistance from members of their family. Some pensioners' adult children supplemented their parents' income by funding specific financial outgoings such as car registration or hospital benefits. For the majority of those relying solely on a social welfare pension, however, life was difficult, with little money available for non-essential commodities.

Some 28 per cent of Irish adults surveyed by Lifetime Assurance in 2000 expected to be relying solely on the state pension in retirement. The figure has been declining over the years but it remains high. Only 13 per cent of 25 to 34 year olds expected to be reliant on a state pension.

'You must be financially secure—even if you are on the pension.'

'I'm on the pension and money dominates my life—I am always worried about money.

'Having enough money is number two after health. Surviving on the pension is terrible—there is no money for the pleasures of life.'

'When you are both on the pension you need to be inter-accountable re spending because money is very scarce. It is galling to have to justify to each other when you want to spend a few cents—you feel like a child again!'

'You need money to pay for things that you are accustomed to.'

Debts after retirement

By far the worst off, financially, were those people who had arrived at retirement still in debt and on a low pension. Trying to manage on a low income while still paying off a mortgage or other debt drove many to despair. The main causes of debt after retirement were:

◆ Debts carried over from a failed business.

◆ Refinanced home loans following a divorce late in life.

◆ Inappropriate credit card usage. This usually occurred where one or both partner's entrenched credit card spending habits were not modified even after their earning power to repay card debits had diminished.

◆ Acting as a loan guarantor for a friend or relative who then defaulted on the loan.

◆ Gambling. This was a growing problem in places where there are high volumes of poker machines spread around the suburbs.

'You need to be financially secure and must have NO debts. Money worries will affect your health.'

'Own your own home—it is essential that it is debt free. Have a secure income source.'

'You can't retire with debts. You can't afford to pay them back.'

'Don't have debts when you retire. Watch your credit card spending—get into the habit of not being a consumer.'

Active financial management

Interestingly, those participants who chose to become involved in the on-going management of their retirement income tended to become very involved. For some of these people, the management of their income became a purposeful activity in itself. The first page of the morning paper to be read came from the financial section, and many used computer software packages to track the performance of their investments.

Maintaining your financial health in retirement

For most people, retirement signals the end of wealth accumulation through salaries or business income. It is now that the important business begins of maintaining your retirement savings and ensuring that they outlast you! This section looks at a number of steps to consider for maintaining your financial health.

Your first steps

Before you seek advice from anyone it is important to spend some time examining your financial needs and goals. You need to be clear about what services you want. Are you seeking advice about one particular investment, or do you want a full financial plan? Are you concerned about estate planning, that is, what happens to your money when you die? Naturally, a good adviser will assist you to clarify these issues. However, in the first instance you should examine needs and goals privately, where you have all the time you like to toss ideas back and forth. During this time, you should also think about how you will control the discussion with the adviser. Always remember that it is your money and you should not just delegate all the responsibility for decision-making to an adviser.

Selecting a financial adviser

Seeking professional financial advice can be a good investment in itself, as there may be ways for you to improve the net income you derive from your investments. For example, a competent financial adviser may suggest that you restructure your financial affairs to legitimately minimise the tax for which you are currently liable, and may possibly suggest an investment that you had never considered.

The process you need to go through to find a good adviser is similar to that for finding a good dentist, doctor or vet. If you do not currently have a financial adviser or have one that you are not satisfied with, you may wish to consider taking these steps:

◆ Ensure that the person you are intending to seek advice from holds the necessary qualifications. In Ireland you can phone the Central Bank on LoCall 1890 200 469 to check that a financial adviser or broker is registered, and to find out the type of advice that he or she is entitled to give. In Britain the Central Financial Services Authority operates a helpline at 0845 6061234. There are various levels of registration. Not all financial advisers or brokers, for instance, are authorised to give a full range of advice on all available products. The majority are not authorised to hold money on a client's behalf.

◆ Ask your friends and relatives about financial advisers they have used and with whom they are happy. It is important to seek recommendations because if you just rely on obtaining names from the Central Bank or Central Financial Services Authority, it is similar to asking the Medical Council for the name of a doctor. Both organisations will put you in touch with people who meet the requirements for registration; however, what they will not and cannot tell you is if the people they suggest are really any good at what they do, or whether they will suit you personally!

◆ Check with the Central Bank or Central Financial Services Authority on their authorisation to provide advice.

◆ Ask them if they have professional indemnity insurance and who their insurer is (if they do not have this insurance, do not deal with them).

◆ Ask the adviser if they provide a free initial session. Go and meet them and during that time form an opinion of them.

◆ Ask them about their practice—see if they are proud of what they do.

◆ Ask them how long they have been in business.

◆ Ask them whether they have clients in similar financial situations to yourself.

◆ Ask what areas they can provide advice on, any limitations on the advice they can provide, and whether they have a bias towards any products in particular.

◆ Ask them how they do their research—look for evidence of current journals and subscriptions to research services.

◆ As you speak with the adviser try to build a picture of their expertise and integrity.

◆ Look at their office and staff—are they enthusiastic and professional?

◆ Most importantly, ask yourself whether you feel comfortable with them. You are the client; if you are not happy with them—leave.

Terms of Business

Ask your prospective financial adviser for a copy of their Terms of Business; all registered financial advisers are required by the Central Bank to have such a document. Financial advisers also have standard Investment Management Agreements that can be varied to suit the client. Both documents provide important information about the adviser, including:

◆ Name and address and details of the authorisation granted by the Central Bank.

◆ What services the adviser offers—can they offer a full planning service, or do they only offer limited advice.

◆ Details of the extent of the discretion to be exercised by the firm.

◆ An outline of the adviser's understanding of the client's investment objectives.

◆ A statement of how the firm expects to be paid for its services.

◆ How the adviser deals with complaints from their clients.

What to expect from a financial adviser

A good financial adviser will include the following steps in their planning process with you:

◆ Gain an understanding of your lifestyle, feelings, preferences, objectives and existing financial plans.

◆ Find out what your tolerance for risk is through identifying your 'risk profile'. This simply means finding out how you feel about high yield, high risk investments versus lower yield, lower risk investments.

◆ Prepare the financial plan in writing.

◆ Conduct a session where the financial plan and recommendations are presented to you.

◆ Address issues beyond income such as estate planning, that is, what happens to your money when you die.

◆ Commence the implementation process where the strategies are put into action.

◆ Establish the need for regular reviews to ensure your plan stays up to date. These reviews need to be tailored to your situation. For some people an annual review is recommended; for more complicated or volatile portfolios, reviews may even be quarterly.

Cost of a financial plan

You should shop around as fees can vary from adviser to adviser. Let them know approximately how much you have to invest and tell them that you need an estimate of the total charges to you. It is important to ask for a total amount because advisers may charge you in a number of ways, for example:

◆ a rate per hour;

◆ a flat fee;

◆ a fee calculated on the amount of money that you invest with them; and

◆ commission based on the financial products you may purchase.

Don't forget that whatever the method of payment, you are paying for good advice. If you find a lower cost adviser, ensure that they are still capable of providing you with the quality of service that you need.

Divulging information to your financial adviser

Once you are dealing with your carefully selected adviser, you will need to provide all the information that you and the adviser regard as necessary to form an accurate picture. They will need to know where you are now financially, where you intend to go financially and when you wish to get there. The type of details you may have to provide include:

◆ your assets;

◆ your daily expenses;

◆ your liabilities;

◆ your present income;

◆ your state of health;

◆ your superannuation and insurance;

◆ your tax liabilities;

◆ your age and that of your partner;

◆ if you are married, whether this is your first marriage;

◆ your goals;

◆ your concerns;

◆ your plans and objectives requiring capital expenditure, for example, holidays;

◆ your preference if you become ill, for example, staying at home under care or moving to a nursing home; and

◆ your intentions for your money on your death.

Do you have a good financial plan?

Does the plan provide all the information that you asked for? If the answer is yes, then you are on the right track. However, you should also review these points:

◆ Make sure that the plan is in writing. It should include information about what is being invested where and why this plan suits your specific needs.

◆ Think about the process that your adviser went through when developing your plan. Did they ask you sufficient detailed questions about your finances and your goals and preferences? Did they appear to be listening, or did they act as if they already 'knew' what you needed? If they committed the unforgivable sin of commencing to sell a product without examining your needs, dump them.

◆ Ensure that YOU have also been totally honest and forthcoming with information. Advisers cannot read your mind, and need to know all about your goals, present financial situation and tolerance for investment risk-taking.

◆ Do you understand what has been recommended and why it has been suggested as a solution for you?

◆ Do you know what the possible trade-offs are? (For example, an annuity provides a guaranteed income but ties up your capital.)

Understanding the jargon

The table below provides a basic list of the jargon you may encounter in retirement-related financial discussions.

Accumulation superannuation fund
An accumulation superannuation fund is one where the employer (and often the employee) contributes an amount to the fund. The benefit on resignation or retirement then is based on the contributions and investment earnings of the fund, less expenses.

Additional voluntary contributions (AVCs)
Extra contributions paid on a voluntary basis into a company pension scheme in order to secure extra benefits.

Annuities
A regular payment made by an insurance company in return for an up-front investment. Pension payments are often annuities. The insurance company guaranteed to pay the pension for life in return for an initial investment.

CGT
Capital Gains Tax is a tax payable on capital gains made on the disposal of an asset.

Defined benefit scheme
A pension scheme where the benefits are defined on the basis of a set formula usually related to years of service and final pay.

Defined contribution scheme
A pension scheme where the benefits depend solely on the amount of money invested and the performance of the fund. They are not related to service or pay.

Index linked

A pension that rises each year in line with inflation or in line with salary increases is said to be index linked.

Retirement lump sum

This usually refers to the tax-free lump sum that can be taken on retirement from a pension fund. The amount is restricted by Revenue Commissioners' rules. An employee may take up to one-and-half year's salary, depending on service, while a self-employed person may take up to 25 per cent of their personal pension fund as a tax-free lump sum. Any amount taken as a lump sum, of course, reduces the amount available to fund a pension.

Avoiding scams, tricksters and desperadoes

Retired people have long been a popular target market for confidence tricksters. Ironically, it is the very need to preserve and maintain their precious retirement savings that leaves some people open to 'get rich' schemes.

Fortunately, there is a government organisation that can check the credentials of companies on your behalf. The Central Bank can be contacted by telephone (LoCall 1890 200 469); or Central Financial Services Authority on 0845 6061234. While they cannot provide advice about the likely performance of a legitimate organisation, they can tell you if the firm is authorised to sell investment products. It is illegal for people selling investment products in Ireland to contact potential clients without first getting their permission. 'Cold calling' is not allowed.

One of the reasons that otherwise intelligent people fall for the schemes of confidence tricksters is that often the investment or scheme appears credible in theory. Conmen and conwomen usually do their homework and understand the desires of their 'market'. On the promise of easy and large returns, investors have been conned into buying anything from diamonds to whiskey stocks. Some of these are scams, but investors have also lost heavily on legitimate investments. There have been many cases of investors losing out badly to commission-greedy advisers by being encouraged to switch investments.

The operator of a seemingly legitimate mortgage and finance bureau in Limerick was found guilty of defrauding 20 investors of a total of £203,000 in amounts ranging from £270 to £97,000.

In Australia a bankrupt lawyer, who was actually in jail as he ran his scam, managed to extract over $1.4 million from eight investors. The scheme centred on convincing the investors that there was a fortune to be made in Canadian Government Treasury Bonds. The crooked lawyer managed to con a former bank manager, a chartered accountant and a stockbroker.

Remember that invariably the higher the advertised return on your investment, the higher the risk, that is, the potential for you to lose your money.

Budgeting

Seek advice from government agencies and financial professionals to determine if there is a better way to structure your assets and invest-ments. If you are over 65 and are not currently receiving a social welfare pension, it is worth checking your entitlement again. The means test applied to savings and investments has been eased in recent years and so too have the contribution requirements for a contributory pension. Remember that social welfare contributions made abroad can be taken into account and in certain circumstances pre-1953 contributions can also be considered.

Draw up a budget and monitor your spending to ensure that you are not letting money slip through your fingers.

The form below contains a breakdown of the types of expenses most of us face during the year. Completing a budget such as this can help you identify your outgoings and may even help you focus on areas where you could make some savings.

	€ per week	€ per month	€ per year
Food			
Alcohol/soft drinks			
Dinners/lunches out			
Groceries—all food items			
Anything else?			
SUBTOTAL			
Accommodation			
Building and contents insurance			
Electricity			
Gas			
Maintenance/repairs			
Mortgage payments/rent			
Local authority charges			
Telephone			
Water rates			
Anything else?			
SUBTOTAL			
Transportation			
Motor insurance and tax			
Driver's licence			
Fuel			
Lease or loan repayments			
Parking fees			
Public transport/taxis			
Registration and third party			
Service/maintenance costs			
Anything else?			
SUBTOTAL			
Health			
Dental expenses (net of benefits)			
Health insurances			
Medical expenses (net of benefits)			
Optical expenses (net of benefits)			
Pharmaceutical supplies			
Anything else?			
SUBTOTAL			

	€ per week	€ per month	€ per year
Personal			
Clothing/footwear			
Entertainment			
Fees			
Gifts			
Haircuts			
Holidays			
Life insurance			
Papers, books etc.			
Recreation and hobbies			
Anything else?			
SUBTOTAL			
Miscellaneous			
Charities			
Pets/veterinary fees			
SUBTOTAL			
TOTAL			

To move or not to move

'Think carefully about relocating—don't make the final commitment straight away. Rent for six months first—you lose communication with family and friends, facilities such as hospitals. You find yourself in a different social environment and a different social pecking order (you stand out!).'

'We moved out of the city—it was great at first because we were able to buy a larger house and a view of the sea. However, we started missing our friends and family terribly and we then found that we could not afford to move back without dropping our standard of housing below what we had before we left.'

One of the most costly mistakes people can make in retirement is to move house without giving sufficient thought to the possible consequences. Sometimes the motivation to move is based on the desire to start a new life that is carefree and full of fun. Work is over, the family has grown up, the children are now independent and the big 'holiday' is about to start. With thoughts like this in mind it can be tempting to leave the old environment behind and start afresh in a new location.

However, just moving down the road will cost you a lot of money. The further you move the higher the removal costs, and these may double if you find that one or both of you cannot adjust to the new area and wishes to return to the old neighbourhood. A further complication arises where people have moved to a lower cost area or state and then find that relocating to their old neighbourhood is now beyond their financial reach.

The following 'fact-finding' questions were suggested by people in the Australian Retire 200 program and from research into the risks associated with moving house after retirement. Therefore, before you move north, south, east or west, take the time to consider these points. Discuss them with your partner—make sure that both of you feel the same way, and that neither of you is under undue pressure from the other to move.

	Yes	No
Is your extended family an important part of your social and emotional life? If so, will moving deny	❑	❑
you sufficient access to them?	❑	❑
Are you the type of person who values the company of old friends from the neighbourhood more than newer friends?	❑	❑
Is the suggested move motivated by the desires of both partners, or is one driving the issue to live in a distant area where, say, the fishing is good?	❑	❑
Will you seriously miss the memories, contacts and history of the house and area in which you presently live? Will the new house/area compensate sufficiently for the loss of these?	❑	❑
How important is the familiarity of the area in which you presently live? Does this familiarity provide you with a sense of well-being and safety that you will miss?	❑	❑

	Yes	No
Is your sole reason for moving based on your inability to maintain your house or to live independently?	❏	❏
If so, your local council or health board may provide subsidised, or even free, assistance when you need to change a tap washer, install a new power point or lop a dangerous tree limb.	❏	❏
Will the new area you are considering have the range of quality services that you may need as you get older?	❏	❏
Is there reliable public transport, a good shopping centre and a range of medical services nearby?	❏	❏
Are there activities and clubs in the area that suit your needs?	❏	❏
Are you being pressured to move because others are trying to tell you to do what they think is good for you?	❏	❏
Have you considered renting for a year and leasing your home out? At least in this way it is possible to come back to your old home in your old neighbourhood if things do not turn out according to your expectations.	❏	❏
Are you succumbing to Moving Mistake 1? *	❏	❏
Are you succumbing to Moving Mistake 2? **	❏	❏

* **Moving Mistake One:** Moving to the town where you have enjoyed your holidays for the last twenty years. The problem with this decision is assuming that the fun you previously experienced there will persist in retirement. Holidays are fun because they provide change from routine, however, if they become the routine they may cease to amuse.

Holiday destinations are also usually associated with circumstances not able to be replicated in retirement. For example, the weather may not be as good in the off season. The nightly visits to others' homes and the regular dining out at restaurants, all of which contributed to your holiday fun, may not be sustainable in retirement.

** **Moving Mistake Two:** The very worst time to decide to move is during or immediately after a time of significant anxiety, depression or stress. As we have discussed earlier, emotional issues arise when we are forced to retire against our will, or when we have lost a partner. Moving at these times can be tempting because it can signify a new beginning. However, for all the reasons mentioned above, the decision to move should be made carefully, calmly and for the right reasons.

CHECKLIST

❏ I have considered the need to use a competent financial adviser.

❏ I have a better understanding of the financial planning process and the jargon used.

❏ I will consider the issues raised about moving house if I decide to move at some time.

❏ I will spend time drawing up a budget to monitor our spending.

References and suggestions for further reading

Costello, John, *Law and Finance in Retirement,* Dublin: Blackhall Publishing 2000.

Directory of Services for Dying, Death and Bereavement, Age Action Ireland, 1996.

Directory of Services for Older People in Ireland, Age Action Ireland, 1994.

Entitlements for the Over 60s, National Social Services Board (now Comhairle), available free from Citizens Information Centres.

Guide to Social Welfare Services SW4. Available from Social Welfare offices.

Kenny, Geraldine, *Take Good Care of Yourself: Growing Older in Ireland,* Dublin: Gill & Macmillan, 1995.

The Law and Older People: A Handbook for Service Providers. Available from the National Council on Ageing and Older People, 22 Clanwilliam Square, Grand Canal Quay, Dublin 2.

Rapple, Colm, *Family Finance,* Dublin: Squirrel Press. An annual guide to all aspects of personal finance.

* * * * * * *

Berne, E. (1961) *Transactional Analysis in Psychotherapy.* USA, Castle Books

Bodger, Carole (1998) *Smart guide to getting strong & fit.* New York, John Wiley & Sons

Bourne, Edmund J. (1995) *The anxiety & phobia workbook.* California, New Harbinger Publications

Ellis, A. & Harper, R. (1975) *A new guide to rational living.* California, Wiltshire Book Company

Harris, T. (1974) *I'm OK—You're OK.* London, Pan Books

Hillman, Carolyn (1992) *Recovery of your self-esteem.* New York, Simon & Schuster

Kidman, A. (1988) *From thought to action.* Australia, Biochemical and General Consulting Service

Laura, R.S. & Johnston, B.B. (1997) *Fit after fifty.* Australia, Simon & Schuster

Monte, C.F. (1977) *Beneath the mask.* New York, Praeger Publishers

Myers, I.B. with Myers, P.B. (1980) *Gifts differing.* California, Consulting Psychologists Press

Myers, Isabel & McCaulley, Mary H. (1985) *A guide to the development and use of the Myers-Briggs Type Indicator.* California, Consulting Psychologists Press

Stanton, Rosemary (1994) *Eating for peak performance.* Australia, Allen & Unwin

Wertheim, E., Love, A., Littlefield, L. & Peck, C. (1992) *I win you win.* Australia, Penguin Books

Appendix A
The 180° Relationship Check

Area	Terrible, ghastly	Needs to improve	Fair to average	Quite good	A saint
My general planning ability					
My money management					
My consideration for my partner's feelings					
My consideration for my partner's need for autonomy and time alone					
My consideration for my partner's need for joint activities with me					
The degree to which I accept responsibility for duties around the home					
The level of empathy I demonstrate when my partner is not well or is sad					
The degree to which I am prepared to bend to attend an outing I will hate but which my partner will enjoy					
The number of little things I do that say 'I love you'					
The level of respect I show for my partner's wishes and opinions					
The manner in which I speak to my partner at home					
The manner in which I speak to my partner in public					
My preparedness to be polite to friends of my partner that I do not like					
The effort I make to be pleasant when I am in a bad mood or upset					
The level of responsibility I take for communicating with our children and grandchildren					

Area	Terrible, ghastly	Needs to improve	Fair to average	Quite good	A saint
My preparedness to answer the telephone when neither of us feels like it					
The level to which we share driving on a long trip					
My sense of humour					
?					
?					
?					
?					
?					

Appendix B
The Decision-making and Task-allocation matrix (DMTA)

List of responsibilities:

1. Deciding where to go for holidays

2. Setting our weekly/monthly budget

3. What colour to paint the house

4. Whether to move house or not

5. What price and style of house to purchase

6. Who looks after the tax returns

7. Who balances our budget

8. Who looks after our savings program

9. Who manages our investments

10. Who pays the bills

11. Who decides on purchases for maintenance, e.g. repairing versus buying a new hot water system

12. Who decides whether to buy new appliances, e.g. the latest TV

13. Who vacuums the house

14. Who cleans the toilets

15. Who decides what we will do today

16. Who decides who we will invite around for dinner

17. Who decides how we will maintain our health

18. Add your own...

CELL A: 100%

(These tasks/decisions are completely mine) e.g. paying the bills.

_____

_____

_____

_____

_____

_____

CELL B: 50–50%

(These tasks/decisions are discussed together and voted on) e.g. where we go for holidays.

_____

_____

_____

_____

_____

_____

CELL C: 75–25%

(These tasks/decisions are discussed together but if we do not agree my partner is the decision-maker) e.g. what colour to paint the loungeroom.

_____

_____

_____

_____

_____

_____

CELL D: 75–25%

(These tasks/decisions are discussed together but if we do not agree I am the decisionmaker) e.g. what brand of television set to buy.

_____

_____

_____

_____

_____

_____

_____

CELL E: 100%

(These tasks/decisions are completely my partner's) e.g. who looks after our tax returns.

_____

_____

_____

_____

_____

_____

_____

Index